HOW TO PROFIT
From
PUBLIC AUCTIONS

Books by Bill Adler, Jr.

The Wit and Wisdom of Wall Street

The Home Buyer's Guide

The Lottery Book

How to Profit from Public Auctions

HOW TO PROFIT
From
PUBLIC AUCTIONS

Edited by Bill Adler, Jr.

WILLIAM MORROW AND COMPANY, INC.
NEW YORK

Library of Congress Cataloging-in-Publication Data

How to profit from public auctions.
    1. Surplus government property—United States—
Purchasing.   2. Auctions—United States.   I. Adler,
Bill, Jr., 1956–   .
JK1661.H68   1989   353.0071'3   88-34510
ISBN 0-688-07088-4

Printed in the United States of America

First Edition

1   2   3   4   5   6   7   8   9   10

BOOK DESIGN BY BRIAN MOLLOY

ACKNOWLEDGMENTS

This book would never have been possible without the skillful prose and hard work of Carol Dana, Tim Wells, and Francine Modderno. Carol, in addition to helping write *How to Profit from Public Auctions*, played a large role in organizing and, when necessary, performing triage on parts of the manuscript. Dana Miller did the early research for *How to Profit from Public Auctions*.

Thanks also go to some nonhuman helpers. Without computers, this book would have taken twice as long to complete and would never have been as comprehensive. Mead Data Central's Nexis data base provided anecdotes and information about government auctions as well as information about federal regulations affecting auctions. Carol, Tim, and Francine each used a different computer and word-processing software. Amazing software let us coordinate two IBM PCs and a Kaypro, and HyperAccess Communications software, Wordperfect, WordStar, and NewWord. The final manuscript was prepared using WordStar.

Contents

INTRODUCTION

Why buy from Uncle Sam? Why bother bidding at public auctions for merchandise that you can just as easily find at Sears Roebuck, 47th Street Photo, or in a Sharper Image catalog? Why go to the extra trouble of researching, driving to auction sites, and bidding to acquire a color television or some other merchandise?

You can "just as easily" find merchandise that's available at government auctions through a mail-order catalog or in a department store. But there is definitely merchandise that is auctioned that is not readily available. You might find a $1,000 antique watch for $300. Or that rare coin you've been looking for to complete your collection. Or three hundred pairs of leather moccasins for $2.50 apiece that you can resell for $25 each. Or a beautiful Porsche. Or a vacation house. Or a regular color television at 50 percent off.

Just about anything you can think of—from office furniture to Jeeps—can be found at government auctions.

Anything lost in the mail, confiscated by Customs or the Internal Revenue Service, or no longer wanted by the Department of Defense can be bought at government auctions.

Why buy from Uncle Sam? Because you can often get great bargains, one-of-a-kind items, large lots of the same merchandise, or something you never knew existed. And you can have fun in the process.

Government auctions are a bargain hunter's dream. Although the various agencies that offer auctions try to get a fair market price, most of the winning bids are for far less than even the deepest discounter can offer. Used cars at government auctions go for hundreds of dollars less than those bought at even the most reputable used-car salesman. Pedigree dogs can go for a couple of dozen dollars.

Many unique and rare items can be found at public auctions. Medical equipment that costs $30,000 sometimes goes for only $100. Coins, stamps, watches, jewelry, autographs, antique musical instruments—things that you can't buy at any price—are available through Uncle Sam.

Retailers love government auctions because they can buy dozens or hundreds of shirts, radios, pens, books— virtually anything—at lower-than-wholesale prices. Many retailers think of the government as the lowest-cost manufacturer of merchandise. And if you're thinking of setting up your own business, there's no better place to look for stuff to sell than at government auctions. So there's substantial profit to be made from government auctions.

Finally, there's serendipity. You never know what's going to turn up at a government auction. There's more variety at auctions than at most local stores. It could be a train set for your son or a microscope for your laboratory that appears unexpectedly at a local sheriff's auction. If you like chance and being pleasantly surprised, government auctions are for you.

But the merchandise aside, our Uncle's auctions are exciting and fascinating. The auction process is no less exciting because the government is the auctioneer. In fact, because it's the Postal Service, Internal Revenue Service, Treasury Department, or Agriculture Department behind the auction block, you know that what's being auctioned won't be boring. What's on the auction block will often be something that some criminal stole (or bought with stolen money), or something you never expected—like an exotic parrot that was confiscated by Customs and now has to be auctioned. Auctions are a great way to spend not only your money but an afternoon.

There's bound to be a government auction near you. Almost every town has sheriff's auctions. The IRS and Customs Service have auctions in most major cities, and so do many other agencies. Some agencies let you bid through the mail. *How to Profit from Government Auctions* will show you where to find government auctions.

Although many government agencies advertise their auctions in newspapers, most people aren't aware of the tremendous bargains and adventure that these auctions provide. Public auctions are like a hidden marketplace or an undiscovered shopping mall—the largest, most diverse shopping mall you've ever seen. But now that you've bought this book, you're armed with all the information you need to shop—for fun or profit.

Bill Adler, Jr.
Washington, D.C.

Part 1

PLAYING THE
PUBLIC AUCTION GAME

1

HOW TO MAKE
THE MOST OF PUBLIC AUCTIONS

Every auction-goer's dream is to walk away from a sale with an "incredible find"—some choice item at an unbelievably low price. And this isn't just a dream: It does happen. There's the case of the sharp-eyed buyer who spotted some sable coats in a batch of "miscellaneous" furs confiscated by the Fish and Wildlife Service. She dropped $15,000 for the lot, kept one for herself, and resold the remainder for $50,000.

If you're quick and sharp—and informed—you can make your own miracles at government auctions.

But auction officials are also quick to tell you that cases like these aren't everyday occurrences. In recent years, the government has become more interested in obtaining a fair return for its merchandise. As a result, officials are making more careful appraisals of items and, in many cases, establishing minimum bids for items. Government auctions are also being advertised more widely, resulting in more bidders—and higher prices—for the items that do go on the block.

But even if you don't "make a killing" at government auctions, you can do very well. Whether your intent is simply to outfit a home office or a business office, to provide the family with a second car, or to obtain merchandise for resale, with some homework, practice, and patience you can get items you want at a price you can afford. Officials say that an experienced auction buyer can obtain merchandise for anywhere from 10 to 50 percent less than the item's market value.

BUYING FOR PERSONAL USE

Government sales can provide you with a wide range of items for personal use: You can find furniture, rugs, TV sets, stereos, cameras, VCRs, bicycles, cars, trucks, land, and houses, as well as unused books, toys, and knickknacks that make excellent gifts.

Household items. Some of the best prices for TV sets, stereos, tape recorders, VCRs, telephone-answering machines, cameras, and other useful household or personal items can be found at local police-department auctions. Much of the merchandise sold at these sales consists of unclaimed stolen goods; they tend to be fairly new and desirable items that thieves thought they could resell quickly.

Postal Service auctions—held to dispose of undeliverable or damaged merchandise—also offer some of the same items, especially the merchandise like stereos, tape decks, and other consumer goods that are commonly shipped by mail. The merchandise at the post office auctions is typically brand new, but buyers at post office auctions often have to purchase merchandise in bulk quantities. So while you might be able to buy a single VCR at a police auction, you'd need to purchase a lot of, say, ten of them at a postal sale.

Clothing and accessories. Customs Service auctions are one place to get good deals on new, imported clothing and shoes (although, since these tend to be sold in large "lots," you may well find quantities are too large for your personal use). U.S. Customs also auctions off the contents of individual suitcases that, for one reason or another, were seized or abandoned at entry points. You'll be gambling on the contents of these bundles, although they can sometimes yield some interesting personal effects purchased abroad.

Because of the growing business in mail-order clothing, you can also often find good deals on wearables at the Postal Service auctions of undeliverable packages.

Probably the best source of watches and jewelry is the auctions held closer to home by local police and sheriff's departments. There you'll find a lot of small but valuable items like the watches, rings, necklaces, and chains that thieves pocketed in local heists. Antique jewelry can sometimes be discovered among assortments of less-valuable costume accessories; if you know what you're doing, you can periodically come away with a valuable find at these auctions.

Toys and gifts. Because so many people purchase gift items by mail, Postal Service auctions are a good source for presents for family and friends. As mentioned earlier, the post office tends to group similar items in large lots, but some toys and other assorted items may be sold separately. Because these items are usually new, they make good bargain gifts.

For good buys on bicycles, it's hard to beat local police-department auctions. Bikes range from older, battered varieties to sleek, lightweight custom models loaded with expensive components. In either case, the prices are well below those you'd pay if you were purchasing the vehicle from a store or private owner. If you're a cycling enthusiast and know the worth of various models, you can do well here. Police auctions are also a good source of inexpensive bikes for your children as they outgrow their present models.

Cars and trucks. Cars are available from a number of different government agencies. General Services Administration (GSA) and Postal Service sales are probably the best source of vehicles for private use, in terms of both cost and reliability.

The vehicles sold by the GSA are from the government fleet—sedans and station wagons, usually fully equipped with automatic transmissions, power steering, power brakes, and air conditioning. The GSA also sells trucks and four-wheel-drive vehicles. Because they were regularly maintained and are generally sold after about six years of use, they tend to be in reasonably good shape (and they should all pass state inspections), so GSA auctions are good places to shop for a second family car or a vehicle for a teenage son or daughter. The government uses pricing guides to establish minimum bids on the GSA models, so there aren't any "steals." But you'll probably pay a few hundred dollars less than you would at a used-car lot, and you may be more likely to get a reliable car in the process, although the government vehicles come with no warranty. As an added bonus, you won't have to listen to an annoying used-car-salesman pitch.

At Postal Service car auctions, you can find the small Jeeps used for mail delivery, as well as the larger panel trucks. Although the age at which the vehicles are sold varies, the Jeeps sold to the public are on average eight years old, and thus are older than the government fleet vehicles sold by the

GSA. However, the Postal Service vehicles that go on the block have all had a tune-up and a fresh coat of paint before the sale. These are often sold at a fixed price which is less than the average retail price listed in standard used-car-pricing books.

At Customs Service, U.S. Marshals Service, and IRS sales, you can often find flashier, and newer, cars—ones that were originally purchased for personal, rather than government, use. Customs ranks right behind GSA in the number of cars auctioned; the models sold through this agency tend to include fancy sports cars or exotic models ordered from abroad or shipped here by people moving back. When the owners fail to claim the auto, to pay duty, or to otherwise abide by import regulations, the car makes its way into official hands and ends up on the auction block. Cars sold by the Marshals Service tend to be private vehicles seized by the Drug Enforcement Agency because the cars were used in the illegal drug trade or purchased with drug profits. Ferraris, Bentleys, and Porsches are among the classier models that have shown up in these sales. As one regular auction-goer says, "The Drug Enforcement Agency always confiscates the best cars." The IRS occasionally seizes and sells expensive cars to settle a tax debt.

By contrast, the vehicles sold by the Department of Defense tend to be quite old and heavily used. The stolen or abandoned cars sold at police-department auctions also have some drawbacks. Like other government merchandise, they are sold "as is," and because the keys for many are missing, you often can't even start up the engine. If you know a lot about cars and enjoy working on them, you can do well at these auctions. But "If you don't know what you're doing, you're better off going to a dealer," one government car-auction official said.

If you do decide to shop for your next car at a government auction, you'll have a better chance of finding a bargain if you:

• consult a used-car pricing book to determine what the average wholesale and retail prices are on any particular model, as well as how any optional equipment on the car affects its value.

• check the tires for depth of tread and signs of uneven wear.

• check the engine oil for cleanliness. (If it's sticky or dark, it might indicate that the oil has not been changed often enough or that it contains an oil additive to reduce excessive consumption.)

• check the transmission stick on an automatic car while the car is running; the fluid should be pink.

• check for new paint on trim or bumper; it might mean the car was in an accident and repainted.

• start the engine or, if auction officials allow, take the car for a short test drive.

• take time between the inspection and sale to check prices on similar models at used car dealers in your area.

Land and property. Ordinary homes, lots, abandoned buildings, and business dwellings are among the properties that can be obtained at government auctions. In addition, in the farm belt, there are some real bargains to be had on family farms whose owners have defaulted on loans. Or, if your taste and pocketbook lean to the more exotic, you might watch for the occasional DEA sales of seized homes of people charged with drug crimes. These properties, which reflect the monied life-styles of their former owners, have included multibedroom mansions in exotic locations, boasting such amenities as poolside bars, multicar garages, private runways, and—not too surprisingly—elaborate security systems. While they aren't necessarily cheap, they tend to hold their value well. As one government official said, "No matter what people pay for them on a deed auction, they'll never get them any cheaper. Did you ever hear of a house like this going down in value?"

Whatever type of property you're considering, take time for a thorough inspection. Residences and dwellings that have been seized by, or have reverted to, the government frequently have been left vacant for long periods and may have problems with deteriorating walls, broken pipes, or infestation. In some cases, land or dwellings may come with some additional strings attached, in the form of mortgages or liens that you may have to assume, or building problems that you will have to correct so that the property will conform with local building codes.

BUYING TO OUTFIT A BUSINESS

Office items. If you're setting up a small business or a home office, government sales can provide you with most of the basic equipment: desks, chairs, typewriters, filing cabinets—even paper shredders! The GSA and the DOD are the biggest sources of office furniture and equipment. But remember that most of the items have seen better days, and most of it wasn't terribly attractive even in its heyday: Desks, chairs and file cabinets tend to be functional metal models that won't win any prizes for design. But if serviceability is what you're after, these auctions are the place to go. Sale prices vary, of course, but officials say you can expect to pay 80 to 90 percent of the piece's appraised value.

BUYING FOR RESALE

Many people shop government sales not just to find items for personal use but to obtain merchandise with resale potential. For example, one post office auction regular buys only packages of cosmetics that got lost en route to drugstores or individual distributors; she resells the makeup to her own clients. A clothes wholesaler picked up several hundred down ski vests at a Customs Service auction for about $8 apiece; they retail for more than $60. Other small merchants use government sales to stock used-car dealerships, bookstores, record shops, junk stores, or flea-market booths.

Certain types of sales and categories of merchandise offer more resale potential than others. Generally, post office and Customs sales are some of the best bets, since the merchandise is usually new and often sold in bulk quantities. Records, books, radios, and cassette tapes are among the items that are commonly sold in bulk at post office auctions. At a Customs auction, a bulk buyer might be able to purchase such varied items as quantities of imported clothes or shoes, bolts of silk fabrics, figurines, leather goods, bottles of wine, or Oriental rugs.

Clearly, the way to make money in merchandise resale is to buy at the lowest prices, then resell the item at a healthy markup. In effect, the government becomes the manufacturer. Those who succeed at this game tend to specialize in one or two categories of merchandise. That way, it's easier to keep track of the going prices for those goods, determine how large the market is, learn who the competition is, and judge the quality of any particular shipment or "bin" of merchandise. With that information in mind, these buyers are in a better position to know what to buy—and at what price—when it comes up at government auction.

How much can you expect to make through resale? Experts say that if you're a buyer who knows your field and who has a steady outlet for the merchandise, you should be able to make a 25 to 40 percent profit on your purchases.

HOW GOVERNMENT SALES WORK

The government uses four different methods to sell its merchandise: auctions, spot bids, sealed bids, and negotiated sales.

Auctions. Government auctions are run much like other auctions. Generally they are held where the merchandise is stored. If there are a sufficient number of items for sale, the agency involved may issue a catalog containing a description of the merchandise; catalogs are sent to people on the agency's auction mailing list, or made available at the viewing preceding the sale and on the day of the sale itself.

Generally, interested bidders are asked to register at the start of the sale. You are assigned a bidding number that will be used to identify you when you make a purchase. Prospective bidders are also often asked to leave a deposit at the start of the sale; the deposit is refunded if no purchases are made or deducted against the total cost of your purchases at the end of the sale. This practice helps prevent people from changing their minds after placing a winning bid and leaving merchandise behind, unclaimed and unpaid for.

Typically, items are brought out and shown to the audience, who make their bids by raising their hands or a numbered paddle, or by calling out a figure. The exception occurs at Postal Service auctions, where goods are not displayed during the auction itself. Instead, to save time, each item or group of items is assigned a lot number and is available for viewing in advance of the sale. During the auction, the auctioneer simply announces the number of the item up for sale and bidding proceeds without the merchandise present.

Most agencies establish a minimum acceptable bid or sale price for merchandise to ensure that the property will generate a reasonable amount of revenue even when the sale price falls short of the market value. Minimums are usually not published, although if that figure is not reached during the bidding, the property will typically be either withdrawn and put up for auction at a later date, or reappraised.

The minimum opening bid suggested by the auctioneer, however, is not necessarily the minimum sale figure that the government will accept. If you're interested in an item, wait and see if someone offers a lower figure than the auctioneer's suggested starting bid, or wait to see if the auctioneer lowers the opening figure.

The bidding then proceeds with the auctioneer boosting the price until competitors have dropped out or the auctioneer decides to move onto the next item. If you are the high bidder, you will usually be asked to pay the purchase price by the close of the sale (although some agencies allow bidders to leave a deposit and pay the remainder when they remove the items). Most agencies allow you some extra time—between twenty-four hours and thirty days—to remove your purchases, especially in the case of large individual items or bulk purchases. Each catalog gives more details on the specific terms of sale.

Spot bids. In some instances, agencies sell merchandise through a spot-bid procedure. These sales operate something like auctions, in that items are shown to an audience of prospective buyers. However, instead of offering a number of progressively higher bids, bidders are allowed to make only one bid on any particular item. The bid is written down on a form provided by the agency. Then the forms are collected and compared with each other as well as with any bids the agency might have received by mail. The person offering the highest figure is awarded the merchandise. The spot-bid approach offers an agency the advantage of being able to move merchandise fairly quickly through a public sale, and also of widening—through the use of mailed bids—the audience for any particular item.

Sealed bids. Sealed-bid sales are conducted almost exclusively by mail and are typically reserved for large, hard-to-move items scattered at warehouses around the country, or for items whose high price tags or specialized use makes them of interest to a narrow buying audience. For example, the Department of Defense might dispose of surplus airplanes through this process, while the Internal Revenue Service might use the sealed-bid approach to sell off a luxury yacht seized to satisfy a delinquent tax debt.

Typically, the agency conducting this sort of sale issues an "invitation for bid," describing the property for sale and its condition and providing information on where it may be inspected. Interested parties submit bids in writing on a special form; usually the bid must be accompanied by a substantial deposit (20 percent of the bid price in many cases) to ensure that the bidder is serious about acquiring the merchandise. Bids remain sealed until a specified date, when the envelopes are opened publicly and the goods awarded to the highest bidder. Deposits for nonwinning bids are returned promptly, usually within fourteen days.

The sealed-bid process offers agencies the advantage of conducting sales by mail, thereby expanding the size of the bidding audience on merchandise of potential interest to a wide geographic area.

Negotiated sales. In cases where an agency has reason to believe that an item has only limited interest to the public at large, agency officials may negotiate directly with a small number of buyers, or sometimes with a single buyer. For example, this method might be used to sell small or oddly shaped pieces of real estate of potential interest only to adjacent landowners, or to dispose of a quantity of scrap metal of interest to only a limited number of salvagers.

CONDITIONS OF SALE

The government offers no warranties or guarantees on its merchandise (although you may be able to void a purchase if you find that the goods were misdescribed in government sales catalogs). Basically, the government is selling its merchandise "as is, where is," and the burden is on you, the buyer, to inspect items carefully ahead of the sale so you'll know just what it is you're bargaining for. The dates and sites for inspection are laid out in catalogs and advertisements for the sales.

Sales catalogs also include information on the conditions of sale. It's worth reading this fine print for details on the terms of your purchase. One typical requirement is that you pay in full for your purchases before you remove them from the premises. Acceptable forms of payment vary according to the agency involved. Most require cash, money orders, or cashier's checks, although the Customs Service recently began to allow the use of credit cards. Agencies rarely accept personal checks.

The government also requires you to make arrangements for removing your purchase, and, as mentioned earlier, most agencies require you to pick up your merchandise no later than thirty days after purchase. So, before you fall in love with that surplus bulldozer or guided-missile launcher, you might want to consider how you'll get it home . . . and where you'll keep it once you do. If you need help moving your purchase, agency sales representatives can provide you with a list of packing and trucking firms.

ADVICE FOR EVERY AUCTION-GOER

Whether you're buying for personal use or possible resale, you'll stand the greatest chance of profiting from government auctions if you follow these tips:

1. Reduce Your Competition. One way to increase your chances of getting a good bargain is to search out sales that draw smaller crowds and fewer bidders. That means attending sales held away from big cities and away from a government agency's regional headquarters. Because of the added travel time and distance from population centers, fewer bidders attend, with the result that there's less competition overall. Sales held on weekdays also generally have smaller crowds than weekend sales. Inclement weather can also reduce the turnout for a sale. Spending three hours under an umbrella at a GSA car auction might just be worth it if you save an additional $500 off the price you'd pay a dealer for the very same car.

2. Examine Goods Carefully Before You Buy. Definitely look before you buy. Government property is sold on an as-is basis, so it's up to the buyer to examine merchandise closely to determine its condition. Most government auctions set up a viewing period in advance of the actual sale. It might be held one or two days before the event, or on the morning of the sale. In any case, set aside enough time to thoroughly examine the items of potential interest, checking them for age and condition. If a catalog is available, be sure the description of the item matches the merchandise, and record your own observations about pieces of interest in the margin. This is also a good time to jot down the amount you'd be comfortable bidding.

It won't hurt to take along a small flashlight, in case the lighting in the viewing room is dim or you find an extraordinary piece hidden away in a dark corner. Some people carry along magnifying glasses to examine pieces closely for cracks, chips, or identifying marks. If you're buying furniture—desks and tables to outfit a small business, for example—take along a tape measure to be sure the items will fit in your available space—and through your doorways!

Custodians present at the inspection can often provide you with additional information about an item, such as its original cost or its age. Don't hesitate to try to find out as much as you can.

Finally, after the viewing but before the bidding, it's a good idea to do additional research on the value of items of interest by checking prices in various guides or retail shops. That'll help you establish bidding limits for yourself.

3. Learn How, and When, to Bid. It's best not to bid on your first sale outing. Instead, attend a few sales—without your pocketbook—just to watch the action and get a feel for the process. Newcomers often get caught up in the auction's excitement and let their emotions and the competitive thrill lead them into paying inflated prices for items they really could do without. Customs auctions officials say newcomers often bid *more* than they would pay at a local store for such items as wine, color TVs, or stereos. A post office auction regular adds: "I've seen people become so competitive they overbid. Once I saw a camera that sells in the stores for $100 go for $115 here."

If you're new to the sale scene, get a seat near the front where you can study the auctioneer, the merchandise, and the other bidders. Keep track of the winning prices in the auction catalog or a notebook. That will give you a reference point that you can use to determine what to bid on similar items in the future. (If you expect to be making purchases at sealed-bid auctions, you can obtain information on past winning bids from the agency in charge of the auction.)

Try to pick out the dealers in the audience—people who consistently bid on one category of merchandise or who buy similar items in quantity. You can learn a lot by watching how dealers play the sale game. For example, notice where they stop their bidding on certain items. Since they must buy cheaply in order to make a profit, their stopping point will give you an idea of an item's wholesale value. (Of course, if you are buying an item for personal use and not for resale, you can often outbid a dealer and still get an item for less than its full market value.)

Dealers can also make life difficult for amateurs, and it's worth being on your guard. Because amateurs and individual buyers can, and will, outbid them, dealers sometimes use a tactic to eliminate this competition. Early in the sale, they'll jack up the bidding on an item they're not interested in and then drop out just before the auctioneer brings down the gavel, leaving the amateur to pay an inflated price. The dealer hopes to "clean out" an amateur's wallet this way, so that later on the newcomers will stay out of the bidding for those items the dealer *really* wants.

You can also avoid competing with dealers by concentrating on single items rather than ones sold in bulk—bidding on a single toy rather than a bin of books at a post office sale, for example—or by going after those items that don't fit the general category of the sale. For example, you might do well if you bid on a case of wine in a Customs sale that drew dealers mainly interested in bidding on large lots of rugs.

When you are ready to go to a sale and enter the bidding, be sure you've examined the merchandise and determined in advance how much you're willing to pay.

At most auction sales, you will be asked to offer your bid by raising a numbered paddle or card, making a hand signal, or calling out the amount you're offering. Don't be afraid to scratch your nose or wave to a friend across the room, though. Professional auctioneers know the difference. And if there is a mistake, any bid can be retracted at any time before the auctioneer brings down the gavel.

4. Remember, This Isn't Your Only Chance. The most important rule in bidding is to stick to your limit. If an item gets away from you, you'll have other chances in the future to bid on similar ones.

TAXES

No matter what you do, you usually can't get away from taxes. And that especially applies to government auctions, because when you buy from one part of the government, other parts, namely the IRS, may know. Taxes are wholly your responsibility. But the good news is that generally taxes aren't significant when it comes to public auctions. If you're purchasing something—say a nice pair of cowboy boots that was confiscated from a drug dealer—you won't have to worry about taxes at all. If, however, you decide to resell the books that you picked up at the Postal Service auction, you must pay tax on the income from the sale (as well as applicable state sales tax). So the rule of thumb is: If the item is for you, you can treat the purchase as a normal retail purchase; if it's for resale, then you must report the income. (Some states charge tax on cars and land; check with your state income tax bureau.)

Part 2

BUYING MERCHANDISE
FROM THE GOVERNMENT

2

GENERAL SERVICES ADMINISTRATION SALES

The General Services Administration (GSA) is the "housekeeper" for the federal government. As such, its duties include buying, selling, and managing the government's possessions. It is the central clearinghouse for almost everything the federal government owns and thus the largest source for U.S. Government surplus.

The GSA was established as an agency-level arm of the executive branch of the U.S. Government under the Federal Property and Administrative Services Act of 1949, expressly for the purpose of managing the government's property and records. Its duties include overseeing the construction and operation of government buildings, procuring and distributing supplies, administering the utilization and disposal of property, organizing government transportation and communications, and stockpiling strategic materials. Among the huge repositories established to store the vast array of goods and records the GSA administers are the National Furniture

Center, the National Tools Center, and the National Archives. The government itself describes the GSA as "similar to a large corporation doing business in a number of different fields."

The GSA's surplus-property sales certainly are big business. The volume of items the GSA unloads each year is staggering. In 1987, the proceeds from its sales amounted to $84 billion, including $100 million in real estate sales and tens of millions in vehicle sales. The GSA's surplus-sales program is the largest single money-making venture of the U.S. Government.

TYPES OF ITEMS AVAILABLE

The GSA's surplus merchandise is as varied as the numerous federal offices and agencies it serves.

The more exotic items the GSA has sold in the last few years include Howard Hughes's "Spruce Goose" airplane, Harry Truman's "Little White House" in Key West, and a number of million-dollar homes in Miami. You can also pick up everyday items like office furniture, computers, and cars, and—if you're in the market—even purchase refuse trucks, scrap metal, and food wastes.

But the GSA is not the place to look for fantastic bargains. Most of what it sells is used, and not much of it is a steal. The GSA's surplus sales are organized to make money for Uncle Sam, and the majority of the merchandise sold goes for 80 to 90 percent of its appraised market value. The GSA contracts with professional appraisers to determine the fair market value of surplus items and seldom accepts bids much lower than what an item would be worth on the open market. Savings, therefore, often are not huge. But what makes GSA sales interesting are the sometimes hard-to-find, and the occasional one-of-a-kind, items.

Three major categories of surplus are sold by GSA: personal property, real property, and stockpiled commodities.

Personal property. In the personal-property category, the GSA sells standard office items such as office furniture, computer equipment, building materials, or vans. In addition, the agency also occasionally auctions consumer items such as precious jewels, luxury homes, and boats or cars, obtained by the government as gifts or through seizures, forfeitures, or abandonment.

Cars comprise a major sub-category of personal property sold by the GSA. In 1986, the GSA auctioned more than 35,000 used vehicles around the country. The GSA also sells airplanes and boats. One of its more interesting auctions was organized in Florida in 1982 to get rid of over a hundred boats of all types seized during the illegal 1980 "boat lift" of 125,000 refugees from the Cuban port of Mariel. The GSA also sometimes sells items from special government collections. A few years back it made $5 million on a sealed-bid sale of Carson City silver dollars of the 1800s.

Among the cream of GSA's auction crop are the occasional Washington, D.C., public sales of "official" gifts received by State Department, White House, or other government employees from foreign nations. To avoid any possibility of bribery, U.S. Government employees aren't allowed by law to keep any official gifts that have a retail value over $165. Official gifts valued at more than that amount may be put on display by the federal government or offered to local governments for their use. But those that

aren't suitable for government use may be bought back by
the recipient for their appraised value. If the official doesn't
want to purchase the gift, then it is destined for the GSA's
auction block. Most of what's sold at these auctions is
high-dollar merchandise. A recent sale, for instance, disposed
of a number of $40,000 Rolex watches given to U.S. officials
by Saudi Arabia. But these sales are irregular, normally held
only once or twice a year, and sometimes less often, depending on how fast the treasure piles up.

Several pages from a recent GSA sales catalog give a
sampling of the items offered in a typical GSA sale.

GSA Surplus Personal-Property Categories

Ammunition, Casings, Reloadable (restricted to licensed
dealers)

Aircraft (includes engines, parts, accessories & support
equipment)

Boats and Marine Equipment

Railroad Equipment

Motor Vehicles, Trailers, Cycles & Snowmobiles

Construction, Mining, Excavating & Highway Maintenance
Equipment

Manufacturing Machinery, Equipment & Supplies

Agricultural Machinery, Equipment, Supplies, etc.

Material Handling Equipment

Buildings' Equipment, Materials & Supplies

Tools & Hardware

Prefabricated Structures

Electrical, Electronic & Communication Equipment, Components, Supplies, etc.

Medical, Dental, Veterinary, & Laboratory Equipment, Instruments, Supplies, etc.

Photographic Equipment & Supplies

Chemicals, Fuels, Gases, & Oils, Related Products & Equipment

Data Processing Equipment & Supplies

Household Furniture, Furnishings & Supplies & Devices

Ores, Minerals, & Other Primary Products

Jewelry, Watches, Clothing, Personal Items, etc.

Food Waste (grease, fat, bones, etc.)

Magnetic Tapes (ADP, audio, video)

Paper (e.g., newsprint, manila cards)

Precious Metals (includes items/materials containing precious metals)

Ferrous & Nonferrous Metals

Textiles (includes leather products & synthetic fabrics)

Waste Oils, Fuels, Lubricants, Chemicals

Salvage/Scrap Vehicles

Other Wastes

Motor vehicles. About 97 percent of the vehicles sold by the GSA are used government cars and trucks. Occasionally, you might also come across some newer vehicles. These include cars bought by the Department of Transportation for testing of safety belts, emission systems, or other government standards, as well as fancier models seized by federal law-enforcement agencies.

The government's fleet is replaced on a regular basis. Sedans and station wagons are typically sold when they're about six years old; the same is true for trucks and four-wheel-drive vehicles. However, sometimes vehicles are disposed of sooner if they've been driven a lot or if maintenance has ceased to be cost-effective. Government vehicles normally have the full range of accessories—automatic transmissions, power steering, power brakes, air conditioning—and have usually been well-maintained. The cars used for testing standards are often a good buy because they have low mileage and normally suffer minimal wear and tear.

As for the confiscated cars, they range from the expensive sports models found in the flashy, big-time, big-business drug world of Miami to broken-down jalopies used by the lower, closer-to-the-ground end of the trade who drive drugs over the Mexican border into the southwestern United States. The GSA once sold several taxicabs confiscated from their owners by the U.S. Border Patrol because they were used to transport illegal aliens. The luxury models sold by the GSA rarely have been involved directly with the commission of a crime. More often they're part of the loot bought with drug money and seized in forfeitures rather than in chases or raids. However, the number of confiscated vehicles sold by the GSA has been declining in recent years as the U.S. Marshals Service has increasingly taken over sales of items obtained as a result of federal law-enforcement efforts.

As with the GSA's other merchandise, its vehicle bargains are in the eye of the beholder. Contrary to popular belief, there are no $50-car steals to be found at a GSA auto sale unless you're buying for scrap. The GSA determines the prices it will accept for auctioned cars by referring to the book values annotated in various used-car guides such as the *Blue Book*. In most cases, what you'll save by purchasing a car through the GSA are the few hundred dollars a dealer would add on commission. However, the government doesn't offer any financing to make it easier for you to drive away.

Real estate. The GSA is also charged with disposing of most of the federal property and buildings that the government no longer needs for its own purposes, or that the government has acquired through other means. For more information on GSA property sales, see Part III.

Stockpiled commodities. The GSA's Stockpile Disposal Division handles sales of precious metals and gems such as silver, diamond and tungsten ore, as well as sales of nonprecious metals and minerals and agricultural materials. Any American—and often foreigners, except when prohibited by Congress—can bid on the government's surplus strategic commodities, although sales are most often of interest to industrial buyers.

The U.S. Government began stockpiling ninety-odd strategic materials in 1946, when the Strategic Materials Stockpile Act was passed, following the adverse experiences caused by materials shortages that threatened the government's ability to wage World War II. The composition of the stockpile changes from year to year, and Congress to Congress, as needs, politics, and technologies change. One item that the GSA's Stockpile Disposal Division has been trying to get rid of for twenty years is the tannin used in processing leather to make soldiers' boots. It seems that the growing popularity of man-made shoe materials and the decline in the U.S. shoe-manufacturing industry have left little market for this particular processing substance.

HOW ITEMS GET ON THE GSA'S AUCTION BLOCK

The Federal Property and Administrative Services Act of 1949 designated the GSA as the agent to dispose of most federal property no longer needed by the government.

In order for federal property to be put on the GSA's auction block, it first has to be declared excess by its "holding" agency. Excess property is any property an individual agency decides it doesn't need any more.

Once property is declared excess, it's reported to the

GSA. Then the GSA determines if any other federal agency has a need for it. If not, it's declared surplus.

But before surplus property is made available to the public, it's first offered for sale to state and local governments "on a fair and equitable basis." After that, nonprofit organizations, charities, and public-service organizations such as schools, hospitals, and public parks have their turn under the GSA's donation program.

What's left, which is quite a lot, is offered for sale to the public.

HOW GSA SALES WORK

Personal-property sales. The GSA conducts both mixed sales and special-category sales of personal property. Anything and everything may be offered in a mixed sale. Special-category sales sometimes are organized for boats, vehicles, and other major items when inventory warrants. Locations with lots of surplus often have special-category sales. In the Washington, D.C., area, for example, one and sometimes two large auto auctions are held monthly.

The GSA's surplus personal property is sold to the public through competitive bidding. The three sales methods used are sealed bid, auction, and spot bid.

A GSA auction is similar to other auctions. Items are shown to an audience of bidders, one by one, while bidders shout their offers. Auctions are advertised publicly, along with a description of items for sale and bidding instructions. If the volume of items to be auctioned is large enough, the GSA will print a catalog, available to anyone who requests it. Those on the appropriate mailing list automatically receive catalogs of upcoming auctions of items in the category for which they've registered.

During the auction itself, items are offered one at a time by an auctioneer. Usually the auctioneer starts with a minimum asking price, based on the item's appraised fair market value. When offers fall below the range the GSA has deemed fair for the item, it is withdrawn from the first round, but it may be offered again later that day or at a subsequent auction. While the GSA's basic asking price will sometimes come down following a reappraisal, items are seldom sold for much less than their fair market value. It's therefore usually futile to underbid, or to wait for an item to be reoffered at a GSA sale.

Sealed-bid sales are conducted mostly by mail. Sales of large, hard-to-move items and of single items are often conducted this way. An invitation for bids (IFB), along with a bidding form, is provided to anyone who contacts the regional office involved. IFBs also go out automatically to those on the GSA's mailing list. The IFB describes the property for sale, special conditions of the sale, when and where the property may be inspected, and when and where bids must be submitted. Sealed bids received at the specified sales office by the date and time indicated in the IFB are opened publicly. Awards are then made to the highest bidder, and the sales office notifies the bidder as soon as possible.

Spot-bid sales are similar to auctions. Items are shown to an audience of prospective buyers one by one, but the bids are written down rather than shouted, and buyers submit only a single bid.

General conditions of sale for GSA surplus goods are laid out in the "General Sale Terms and Conditions" (Standard Form 114C). Copies of SF114C can be obtained from any GSA customer-service bureau. Special conditions of sale apply to certain classes of property, such as cars that don't conform to U.S. pollution standards. These conditions will be laid out in bid announcements and catalogs.

Dates and sites for inspecting items on sale are indicated in catalogs and ads. Usually, inspections are on the day before, and on the morning of, the sale. Prospective bidders sometimes have to register in advance of a sale. A valid driver's license usually is required to register for auto auctions.

There are no warranties or guarantees on GSA property. Therefore, it's crucial that you inspect items before bidding. Deficiencies in merchandise will be mentioned in the sales brochure—*if* the GSA is aware of them. But just because a deficiency isn't noted doesn't mean there aren't any, and lack of any listed deficiency will not void or change your contract if you do find one after you buy an article. Under certain circumstances you may be able to get your money back, but only if the item has been blatantly misdescribed. The government does warrant to the original purchaser that "the property listed in the invitation for bids will conform to its description." If a misdescription is determined before removal of the property, your money will be refunded. If you take the property away and find an obvious misdescription, you might be able to get a refund if you submit a written notice to the contracting officer within fifteen calendar days. The GSA will not make refunds for shortages of property sold in lots.

Successful bidders may not remove any property until payment in full has been made. In the case of items sold for over $1,000, deposits sometimes will be accepted at the end of a bid, but the merchandise may not be removed from GSA premises until paid for in full.

Acceptable forms of payment for GSA surplus personal property are cash, money orders, traveler's checks, cashier's checks, credit-union checks, or government checks. Personal checks are accepted only when accompanied by informal bank letters guaranteeing payment to the U.S. Government up to a specific amount. The letter also must say that the check covers the purchase of U.S. Government property *only*. Letters are good for a maximum of thirty days and must be approved by the GSA auctioneer before the sale. All checks must be one-party checks.

Surplus stockpiled commodity sales. Many stockpiled commodities, among them industrial diamonds, are sold by sealed-bid auction to the highest bidder. But most are sold in huge lots that usually are of interest only to industry purchasers. A recent offering of tin, for example, was sold only in five-metric-ton parcels. All surplus commodities that go on sale are assigned a minimum acceptable price by the government. The tin offering mentioned above was priced by the GSA at $3.19 per pound, which added up to over $35,000 per purchase.

Sales of stockpiled commodities also are rationed so that no purchaser can obtain a monopoly on a particular item. In the case of the tin, the offering was parceled out over time— not all of it was sold at once. Also, this particular offering was sold according to a preset price—the tin was not auctioned.

The GSA also sometimes sells surplus commodities on the commodity futures exchanges, although this is rare, due to the government's cash-basis policy.

HOW TO FIND OUT ABOUT GSA SALES

The GSA conducts both local and regional sales. Announcements of upcoming sales are made by the regional office involved. All GSA sales are advertised in the U.S. Commerce Department's newspaper, the *Commerce Business*

Daily. They're also advertised in local, regional, or national commercial newspapers, depending on how wide the GSA determines the interest may be. Occasionally, they're advertised in commercial papers abroad. American papers that carry announcements of major or interesting sales include the *New York Times, Washington Post, Boston Globe, Miami Herald, Chicago Tribune,* and the *Los Angeles Times.* Many Canadian papers also frequently carry announcements of major GSA sales. You'll have to browse these papers carefully, because auction advertisements can appear in any sections, including classifieds.

The best way to stay updated on coming GSA sales is to get your name on one, or several, regional-office mailing lists. Those on a mailing list receive sales catalogs and announcements regularly. Separate mailing lists are maintained by each region. Each region also maintains separate mailing lists for personal property and real property. Just write the office handling each region or category of goods you're interested in and ask them to send you an application for their surplus personal property mailing list and/or their surplus real property list. They'll send you a large, post card-type of form on which you write your name and address and check off categories and locations of property you're interested in. The GSA's mailing lists are purged on a regular basis. If you don't submit a bid after receiving five catalogs, your name will be removed from the list. To get back on, you'll have to request a new application. The addresses for the regional offices are listed below.

Info on sales of personal property. Some GSA regional offices have a 24-hour telephone recording announcing sales in the coming month. The numbers for those recordings are listed with the addresses of GSA customer-service bureaus below.

GSA Customer Service Bureaus

GSA has customer service bureaus across the United States. Sales of personal property are divided into ten regions. The addresses, and the states and areas served by each, are given below. For information and or to be placed on a region's mailing list for sale announcements and catalogs, write Surplus Sales, Customer Service Bureau, U.S. General Services Administration, at the appropriate location. For notification about the GSA's occasional sales of official gifts from foreign countries, you'll need to be put on the National Capital Region list.

Region	Areas Served
National Capital Region 7th & D Streets, S.W. Washington, DC 20407 (202) 557-7796 (recording) (202) 577-7785	Washington, DC, metropolitan area, including nearby Maryland and Virginia
Region 1 Post Office & Courthouse Boston, MA 02109	Connecticut, Maine, Massachusetts, New Hampshire, Rhode Island, Vermont
Region 2 26 Federal Plaza New York, NY 10278	New Jersey, New York, Puerto Rico, Virgin Islands
Region 3 Ninth & Market Streets Philadelphia, PA 19107	Delaware, Pennsylvania, West Virginia, Maryland, Virginia (except for Washington, D.C., metropolitan area)

Region 4
75 Spring Street, S.W.
Atlanta, GA 30303

Alabama, Florida, Georgia,
Kentucky, Mississippi,
North Carolina, South
Carolina, Tennessee

Region 5
230 S. Dearborn Street
Chicago, IL 60604
(312) 353-0246 (recording)

Illinois, Indiana, Michigan,
Minnesota, Ohio, Wis-
consin

Region 6
1500 Bannister Road
Kansas City, MO 64131

Iowa, Kansas, Missouri,
Nebraska

Region 7
819 Taylor Street
Fort Worth, TX 76102

Arkansas, Louisiana, New
Mexico, Oklahoma, Texas

Region 8
Bldg. 41-Denver
Federal Center
Denver, CO 80225

Colorado, Montana, North
Dakota, South Dakota,
Utah, Wyoming

Region 9
525 Market Street
San Francisco, CA 94105
(415) 974-9189 (recording
for Northern California)

Arizona, California,
Commonwealth of the
Northern Mariana Islands,
Guam, Hawaii, Nevada

(213) 267-6753 (Southern
California)

Region 10
GSA Center
Auburn, WA 98002

Alaska, Idaho, Oregon,
Washington

The GSA puts out a booklet, "Sale of Federal Surplus Personal Property," which you can obtain free from your regional GSA office or from the General Services Administration, Office of Federal Supply and Services, Washington, D.C. 20406. The GSA will automatically send you a copy when you write to be placed on any of its mailing lists for announcements of personal property surplus sales.

Copies of the Federal Acquisitions Regulations can be obtained from the Office of Acquisition Policy, General Services Administration, Room 4037, 18th & F Streets, N.W., Washington, D.C. 20405, (703) 523-4862. Copies of Federal Property Management Regulations can be obtained from the Office of Regulations Management Division, Crystal Mall, Building 4, Federal Supply Service, GSA, Room 1941, Jefferson Davis Highway, Washington, D.C. 20406, (703) 557-7990.

If you're really into buying vehicles from the government, you might be interested in the GSA's annual report on the federal motor vehicle fleet, which contains detailed data on GSA vehicles. Write National Travel and Transportation Regulations Division, Office of Transportation, General Services Administration, Crystal Mall, Building 4, Room 5, Washington, D.C. 20405, (202) 557-1253.

Those with a keen interest in the GSA's occasional auctions of official gifts and awards from foreign nations can consult the annual list of official awards and gifts published in the *Federal Register*. The list includes a full description and estimated value for each item. Questions about items may be sent to the U.S. Department of State's Office of Protocol, at 2201 C Street, N.W., Room 1238, Washington, D.C. 20520, (202) 647-0907.

For information about the GSA's donation program, contact the Donation Division, Office of Property Management, GSA, Washington, D.C. 20406, (202) 557-1234.

Info on sales of stockpiled commodities. Only one central mailing list is maintained for the GSA's stockpiled commodity sales. The sales are administered by the Stockpile Disposal Division, located in Washington, D.C. To place your name on the mailing list, contact Stockpile Disposal Division, Federal Property Resource Services Administration, Room 5221, 18th & F Streets, N.W., Washington, D.C. 20405, (703) 535-7225.

3

POST OFFICE SALES

The U.S. Postal Service is in the business of conducting public auctions in spite of its desire not to. "What we would like to do as much as possible," said a Postal Service representative, "is eliminate these auction sales."

The Postal Service would much prefer to deliver *all* of the parcels it receives to their rightful owners. But every year the Postal Service is saddled with vast quantities of undeliverable mail that includes a tremendous amount of valuable merchandise. The end result is that the agency is forced to the auction block, and the interested buyer is rewarded with some of the most entertaining auctions to be found anywhere in the United States.

Every month, the U.S. Postal Service finds itself in possession of thousands of valuable parcels that it is unable to deliver because of torn packaging, missing address labels, or improper addresses. The Postal Service routinely places these parcels in its dead-letter bin, where they are kept for six months in order to give customers an opportunity to claim their property. More often than not the property remains unclaimed, and these items are then put up for auction.

Another source of Postal Service auction items is merchandise insured by the Postal Service but damaged in transit. Upon payment of the insurance claim, the post office automatically becomes the owner of the damaged merchandise. All salvageable property is kept for resale.

Postal Service auctions do not offer an opportunity to purchase celebrity belongings, rare works of art, or exotic automobiles. But a surprisingly wide range of merchandise is regularly put on display by the Postal Service, and buyers report that tremendous bargains can be found. In fact, one of the major attractions of post office auctions is that it is impossible to predict what will be put on the block. Said one buyer at a recent New York auction, "It's a joy of discovery. You really can't go wrong because it's so much fun."

TYPES OF ITEMS AVAILABLE

As a rule of thumb, popular gift items are among the most common pieces of merchandise sold at these auctions. A buyer can always be sure of finding generous supplies of toys, records, cassette tapes, books, clothing, jewelry, cosmetics, kitchenware, and decorative household items such as Oriental elephants and brass ducks. But the supply is by no means limited to gifts and trinkets, and a few surprises are always in store. "Anything that is mailable, we get," explained the New York superintendent of claims, who said that a full suit of armor and a large, collapsible boat were among the items included in recent auction collections.

Virtually all of the merchandise recovered from parcels

assigned to the dead-letter bin is brand new, and because it has never been used it is in excellent condition. However, the quality of items damaged in transit varies greatly, and buyers are cautioned to examine this merchandise carefully prior to tendering a bid. Damaged merchandise is identified as such and separated from other goods at the auction.

HOW POSTAL SERVICE AUCTIONS WORK

In years past, numerous local post offices scattered across the country auctioned off the merchandise they accumulated at irregular intervals. However, in order to streamline this process, the Postal Service has recently divided the country into five different regions, and within each region a single post office has been designated to sell all of the dead-letter parcels and damaged merchandise that is acquired in that region. The five cities that currently conduct Postal Service auctions are New York, Philadelphia, Atlanta, St. Paul, and San Francisco. In New York and San Francisco, general merchandise auctions are held every month. The post offices in the three other regions hold their auctions less frequently, and average between six and ten auctions per year.

Prior to attending a post office auction, potential buyers should be aware that all items are sold from a catalog and are *never* put on display in the auction room. All viewing must take place prior to the auction. Inspection of merchandise is permitted from 9:00 A.M. to 4:00 P.M. on the day prior to the auction, or from 9:00 A.M. to 10:30 A.M. on the morning of the public sale. Upon registration for viewing, each buyer is provided with a free catalog that lists all of the items up for sale. Buyers are allowed to keep the catalog and are encouraged to make notations in it for use during the auction proceedings.

One of the special features of a Postal Service auction is that similar types of merchandise are collected in large bins whose entire contents must be purchased at once. The discriminating shopper does not have the opportunity to purchase a single record album or a good book but finds that such items are being sold in bulk lots. A typical bin might include such things as: 750 paperback books; 200 hardback books; 500 men's shirts; 500 cassette tapes; 15 portable radios; or 10 television sets. A minimum bid of $20 is placed on every bin.

When the auction is brought to order, the auctioneer begins by calling out the numbered lots listed in the catalog. The Postal Service uses the paddle system, wherein registered buyers are given numbered paddles on entry. To place a bid, the bidder simply raises the paddle. Because no merchandise is put on display, the post office auctions move at an incredibly rapid pace, with 100 to 150 lots being sold every hour during the four or five hours that it takes to run an auction. To prevent any conflicts of interest, neither Postal Service employees nor their surrogates are allowed to tender bids.

The Postal Service does not accept personal checks unless your name is registered on the approved-checks list made available to regular buyers. Otherwise, payment must be made in cash or by certified check or money order. Payment is expected upon acceptance of the winning bid and must be made prior to the close of the auction.

Regional post office auctions bring in as much as $40,000 or $50,000 per session. The money is retained by the Postal Service and is incorporated into its operating budget, where it is used to help defray the costs of processing claims on damaged parcels.

TIPS FOR POSTAL SERVICE AUCTION SHOPPERS

Over the course of the past decade, Postal Service auctions have become increasingly popular and usually attract between 250 and 400 buyers per session. The bidders include a large number of professional buyers interested in purchasing items for resale, as well as individual shoppers in search of a bargain. The practice of selling merchandise in bulk quantities is attractive to professional buyers, and they tend to make up more than 50 percent of the bidding audience. "Most of the buyers have resale outlets for the merchandise they buy," said Al Thompson, the superintendent of claims at the St. Paul post office. "We get a lot of people who attend these auctions on a regular basis, and some of them come from as far away as Florida or Arizona. For them it's part of a regular circuit they make, and we get to know them on a first-name basis." Such buyers frequently include the owners of secondhand bookstores, record stores, and junk shops, and merchants who resell items at flea markets.

The presence of these merchants guarantees that the bidding will be competitive for those items sold in bulk quantities. However, the casual shopper in search of a bargain should not despair. In addition to the items sold together in lots, a buyer can find a good selection of items sold individually. This happens in cases where the post office hasn't accumulated enough of that category of goods to sell it in bulk, or in cases where an individual item—say, an expensive coat—might bring high enough bids to justify selling it by itself. A retired citizen who regularly attends the Postal Service auction in New York to purchase toys for his grandchildren explained, "The buyers who sell to stores aren't interested in small quantities, but I am." Frequently, the bidding tends to be less competitive on those items that are not sold in bulk quantities, and it is here that the best bargains can be found.

Items that have been damaged in transit can also provide excellent opportunities for bargain hunters. This is particularly true for the mechanically inclined shopper who is willing to make the necessary repairs. Often the replacement of a small part can make a television set or an electronic appliance as good as new. All damaged merchandise is identified as such, and items that are not salvageable for resale are destroyed. "If we put out a bunch of junk," explained the superintendent of claims in St. Paul, "people would be hesitant to come back and buy a second time. We do plug in television sets to make sure they work, and do our best to let potential buyers know what sort of damage has been done. We never try to fool anybody." Still, he cautions that merchandise is sold in as-is condition, and all sales are final. A regular auction attendee says, "You never know with the mechanical items. It's always a risk. But that's part of the game."

HOW TO FIND OUT ABOUT POST OFFICE AUCTIONS

The best way to find out about upcoming Postal Service auctions is to get your name on the mailing list(s) of the regional post office(s) that are of interest to you. The post office mails its notices ten to fourteen days prior to the sale. Public notices are also displayed at local post office branches near the auction site. The agency is permitted to advertise its auctions in newspapers, but rarely does. In San Francisco, the regular general merchandise auction is held on the third Thursday of every month. In New York, the auctions are always held on Tuesdays, with Monday set aside as a viewing day, but there is no guarantee which Tuesday of the month will be chosen as the auction date. To have your name placed on a post office mailing list, simply write or call any of the regional post offices listed below:

Superintendent of Claims, Inquiry, & Undeliverable Mail
U.S. Post Office
J.A. Farley Building
New York, NY 10199-9543
(212) 330-2932

Superintendent of Claims, Inquiry, & Undeliverable Mail
U.S. Post Office
Philadelphia, PA 19104-9597
(215) 596-5544

Superintendent of Claims, Inquiry, & Undeliverable Mail
U.S. Post Office
St. Paul, MN 55101-9514
(612) 293-3083

Superintendent of Claims, Inquiry, & Undeliverable Mail
U.S. Post Office
Atlanta, GA 30304-9506
(404) 765-7309

Superintendent of Claims, Inquiry, & Undeliverable Mail
U.S. Post Office
1300 Evans Avenue, Room 291
San Francisco, CA 94188-9651
(415) 550-5400

SPECIAL POST OFFICE AUCTIONS

In addition to its regional general-merchandise auctions, the Postal Service also conducts three or four special auctions during the year. A huge number of books are shipped through the mail, and even though books are regularly sold at the general merchandise auctions, the Postal Service regularly finds itself stuck with large inventories. In order to deplete this stockpile, the Philadelphia post office holds a special book auction two or three times a year. As is the case in the general merchandise auctions, all books are sold in large bins that average 750 paperbacks or 200 hardbacks per bin. Included in these collections are a large number of how-to books, home-repair manuals, religious books, and thousands upon thousands of cookbooks. The special book auctions are designed to appeal to buyers who have resale outlets, such as the owners of secondhand bookstores. The same rules apply that are used in the general merchandise auctions. All bidding is done from a catalog, and a minimum bid of $20 is placed on each lot. The winning bid frequently runs as high as $200 per bin.

The Philadelphia post office maintains a separate mailing list for individuals interested in the special book auctions. To have your name placed on the list, contact the Superintendent of Claims, Inquiry, & Undeliverable Mail, United States Post Office, Philadelphia, Pennsylvania 19104. Notices are mailed out approximately two weeks prior to the scheduled auction date.

The post office also auctions off surplus vehicles at special sales throughout the year. The Postal Service regularly upgrades its fleet of delivery vehicles, and when it does so a large quantity of used right- and left-hand-drive Jeeps and one-ton trucks are made available to the general public.

Unlike other Postal Service auctions, surplus vehicle sales do not attract large numbers of resale buyers. The audience is made up of one-time buyers in search of a good deal, and those who have attended one of the Postal Service's surplus vehicles sales report that attractive prices are often available.

Prior to making its surplus vehicles available for sale, the Postal Service sees that each car and truck is given a tune-up and a fresh coat of paint. Inspection is permitted prior to the sale, and arrangements can usually be made for a test drive or two. Many of the vehicles are sold at a fixed price rather than through competitive bidding, and all sales are final. Payment must be made in cash or through a certified check or money order, and is expected at the time of purchase. The Postal Service offers no minimum warranties, and the purchaser is responsible for any mechanical failures that arise subsequent to the sale.

Surplus vehicle sales are conducted by various fleet-management offices throughout the country. They are always advertised in the local newspaper, and notices are usually posted in nearby post offices prior to the sale. Mailing lists are maintained. In order to find out the location of the regional fleet management offices responsible for surplus vehicle sales in your area you can write to: U.S. Postal Service, Office of Fleet Management, Room 7246, 475 L'Enfant Plaza, Washington, D.C. 20260.

4

U.S. CUSTOMS SERVICE SALES

The job of the U.S. Customs Service is to collect revenue from duties and fees on imports, and to enforce customs and related U.S. laws. That job entails assessing as well as collecting duties, excise taxes, fees, and penalties on imported merchandise; interdicting and seizing contraband; processing persons, carriers, cargo, and mail into and out of the United States; administering certain navigation laws; and detecting and apprehending persons engaged in fraudulent practices designed to circumvent customs laws or other U.S. laws and regulations pertaining to exporting and importing goods. Customs works closely, in particular, with the Drug Enforcement Administration. It also works closely with the Commerce and Agricultural departments to compile trade statistics.

The area administered by the U.S. Customs Service is divided into nine customs regions throughout the fifty states and the Virgin Islands and Puerto Rico. Within these regions are forty-six subordinate district area offices and approximately three hundred ports of entry to the United States.

Until recently, each of these ports held its own periodic auctions of abandoned or seized goods, but in the late 1980s Customs decided to get out of the auction business and concentrate its efforts on law enforcement. In 1985 it contracted out management of its auctions to a subsidiary of Northrop Worldwide Aircraft, which has consolidated the sales and set up two main auction centers in Newark, New Jersey, and Los Angeles. Although Customs auctions still are held throughout the country, fewer districts are involved.

Northrop's contract does not award it any commissions on the sales. All the proceeds go to the U.S. Treasury, although the government has to hold them for two years in order to satisfy any liens that may be claimed on property sold.

TYPES OF ITEMS AVAILABLE

Customs has quite an assortment of goods, mostly personal property, but also real property if the latter has been bought with proceeds from smuggling. Two categories of personal property are auctioned through Customs: 1) property that's seized or forfeited because either it or its entry is illegal; and 2) merchandise that has been placed in public stores or a bonded warehouse when an improper, but not necessarily criminal, entry has been attempted. The latter category is termed "general order" property and usually consists of goods that have been ordered by American merchants from abroad for sale in the United States. General-order merchandise goes on the auction block after it has remained in custody for one year.

Customs does not sell any of the contraband goods it confiscates. U.S. law requires that contraband, such as drugs or pirated copies of copyrighted American goods, be destroyed. When a piece of equipment, such as a computer, contains only one pirated part, Customs often will remove the pirated part and sell what's left.

. Most of what Customs sells is unusual, and much of it is brand new. You'll find foreign wines, Oriental rugs, leather goods, silks, furniture, figurines, fancy cars, even luxury homes—you name it. And there are some real bargains to be had, even among the not-so-new, because the variety of merchandise is so huge that Customs can't find enough knowledgeable appraisers to evaluate it all.

That wide variety of merchandise usually works to the advantage of buyers. In one such instance, the Los Angeles Customs district auctioned a box of dirty, assorted Chinese earthenware that it considered junk worth no more than about $100. The auctioneer was puzzled when he elicited a bid of $900 for the box, but he didn't give it much thought because people often get carried away in the treasure-hunt tension of a Customs auction. After the sale, the beaming buyer came up and told the auctioneer he was an archaeologist. He said he'd lain awake in excitement all night after the presale inspection, praying no one else had eyed the box he'd literally tripped over by accident. The "junk" he blissfully walked away with turned out to be priceless ancient Chinese pottery.

Personal property. The majority of the goods Customs auctions off were ordered from abroad by U.S. companies, either for sale in the United States or for some other business use. Often companies abandon goods simply because a sale has been lost between the time they placed the order with an overseas supplier and the time the order was delivered at a U.S. port; the companies simply do not want to pay the duties on merchandise they can't sell.

Sometimes large commercial orders are confiscated because of quota restrictions. U.S. trade regulations put strict annual limits on the quantities of many goods allowed into this country, particularly textiles, because of the competition they pose to U.S. manufacturers. These quotas are assigned by country of origin and category of goods. The categories, which are fairly detailed, are negotiated regularly between the U.S. trade representative and individual foreign countries, most under the Geneva Agreements on Tariffs and Trade (GATT). A U.S. buyer who doesn't get an order into the United States before the quota runs out on the category of goods being imported won't be allowed to claim it from Customs. And usually it isn't worth the expense for the buyer, or the supplier, to ship the order back to the country of origin, so it ends up on Customs' auction block.

Customs also sells many souvenirs brought into the United States by travelers who didn't have the money to pay the duties required, didn't have the proper papers, or didn't follow the proper entry procedures.

Travelers frequently try to bring in things that aren't obvious contraband but that are nevertheless restricted due to certain U.S. policies. Certain furs fall into this category as the government considers the animals endangered species. Because they aren't really dangerous to the public or don't threaten U.S. copyrights, these items also wind up on the Customs auction block.

Merchandise associated with illegal-entry crimes that Customs has previously auctioned off include two dozen jewel-studded watches that belonged to the famous Indian guru Bhagwan Shree Rajneesh. Customs seized the watches, some of them valued at $40,000, before Rajneesh was ordered out of the United States in 1985 for immigration fraud.

More mundane examples of items put in Customs auctions are the 24,000 assorted cartons of toys auctioned off in San Francisco in May 1988, and the 6,000 pounds of new bar mops auctioned off in Philadelphia the same month.

And the kinds of prices you might pay for Customs merchandise? Here are some examples of selling prices for items in a 1985 Buffalo auction: A lady's watch and fifteen gold chains, with an appraised value of $4,100, went for $1,225, and a crystal chandelier with an appraised value of $750 went for $575. In a New Orleans auction the same year, two diamond necklaces valued at $1,700 sold for $800. A 3.28-carat diamond valued at $13,600 went for $9,200 in a Honolulu auction that year. And in a San Diego auction in 1987, a brand-new bamboo bedroom set sold for $275, ninety-six water heaters sold for $2,300, a ceiling fan sold for $25, and two cartons of cups and mugs went for $30, according to the *Los Angeles Times*.

Among the "hottest" merchandise at Customs auctions is clothing. Clothing and personal effects that have been abandoned in suitcases by individual travelers are particularly popular with the flea-market crowd. All the effects in a suitcase normally are bound together and sold as one item. Bidding on these bundles can sometimes get frantic because buyers often think they may find hidden treasure in the effects. What they don't seem to know is that Customs searches these bundles first and removes any precious jewels or other valuables before selling them. The heat of the treasure-hunt atmosphere drove up the price on one such bundle auctioned in Los Angeles to $1,500. After the auction, a crestfallen man came up to the auctioneer and said the items just sold had been his—he'd abandoned the suitcase because he didn't want to pay the $100 or so duties assessed. He'd waited and watched the Customs auction schedules in hopes of retrieving his things. He said the items in the suitcase had little worth other than sentimental value. The auctioneer told him to hang around until the winning bidder had gone through the effects, then offer him $50 for the lot. He said the bidder no doubt would be glad at that point for the offer.

One of the more curious categories of items Customs sells is tropical birds. Huge numbers of birds are seized by Customs along the U.S.-Mexican border, and Texas, in particular, is the venue for frequent bird auctions. Most of the birds are rare, endangered species prohibited for import into the United States. However, once the birds are here, Customs usually sells them, rather than destroying them or attempting to return them to their point of origin. Among the creatures that show up in the inventory are exotic varieties such as Mexican redhead Amazon parrots, Senegal parrots, and lilac-crown conures. In Hawaii, Customs collects lots of precious gems to auction off. Along the seacoasts, it collects boats to sell. And in the northeast, it auctions a large number of Franklin stoves.

Vehicles. Customs is second only to the GSA in the number of autos it auctions off. And Customs' cars are the pick of the government lot, as most of them were originally bought for personal use. You're more likely to find fancy sports cars, vintage autos, or exotic foreign models among Customs' inventory. Some of Customs' cars were shipped here by individuals moving from another country, some are new cars ordered from abroad, some are cars that have been used to transport contraband or illegal immigrants.

Customs' foreign cars sell well below U.S. prices, but there are hitches to watch out for. According to one estimate, about two thirds of Customs' cars are seized because they don't meet U.S. safety or environmental standards. Unfortunately, these cars, labeled "for export only," can't be driven in the United States as is. They must be either exported after purchase or adapted to U.S. standards, which can take the bargain out of the purchase. The cost involved in modifying one of these cars to meet U.S. standards could outweigh what you save on the purchase price. However, by modifying an "export only" car, you can obtain an automobile that is rare in the United States.

One such "bargain" that was sold at a Miami Customs auction in 1981 was a 1972 Rolls Royce convertible appraised at $140,000. The Rolls was seized in 1976 after the British woman who imported it abruptly left the United States without paying the $698 duties she owed on the car. The winning bidder got it for $27,000. However, the car needed new brakes, a new convertible top, a paint job, a new windshield, and work to enable it to comply with U.S. emission standards. The winning bidder estimated the repairs would cost him between $7,500 and $20,000. Nevertheless, he thought he got a remarkable buy.

Customs sells a lot of airplanes and boats, most of them seized because they're used to smuggle drugs. One retired couple picked up a 45-foot, 17-ton, two-masted fiberglass yacht in South Carolina that had been seized with 4,000 pounds of Colombian marijuana on board. Their winning bid was $41,500—a full $13,000 less than the government's appraisal. How did the couple arrive at their bid? They looked at ten similar yachts, determined their average price, then divided by half. After repairs, many of which they did themselves, the couple figured their boat was worth more than $175,000. Their name for their bargain? *Pot Luck*.

Occasionally Customs doesn't clean out all of the contraband stashed aboard the vehicles it sells. In one such instance in 1984, a 56-foot fishing boat was auctioned off in Mobile, Alabama, with a load of 3,100 pounds of marijuana worth $2 million on board. The boat had been seized in the Gulf of Mexico by the Coast Guard in September 1984 and turned over to Customs in Gulfport, Mississippi. Although they had removed part of the marijuana on board, Customs officials overlooked sixty-two burlap-covered, 50-pound bales of the drug that had been hidden inside compartments below deck. The new owner handed over the boat's hidden cargo to Customs as soon as he found it.

HOW CUSTOMS AUCTIONS WORK

U.S. Customs is the only one of the major federal auctioneers that has privatized its sales. Customs contracted the job to Northrop in 1985, not only to get itself out of the auction business but so that taxpayers could make more money on sales of the goods it collects. Once run on the GSA model, Customs auctions now are run using commercial auction procedures.

One of the conditions of the Customs-Northrop agreement is that Northrop advertise the sales to potential end-users, i.e., industries that may be interested in particular categories of goods. Advertising for sales of aircraft parts, for instance, would be targeted to aircraft manufacturers. In the past, many of the bidders at Customs auctions were middlemen, who purchased goods for the purpose of selling them to end-users. The new practice probably will reduce the number of middlemen who participate in Customs auctions. Relatively few people knew about Customs auctions before, which kept the competition down and increased one's chances of coming away with a bargain, but prices should creep up as Northrop's advertising campaign gathers more, and more serious, bidders. Legally, the only limitation on the bottom price you can bid on Customs goods is the duty owed on the merchandise, but again, Northrop's more sophisticated sales campaign undoubtedly will drive up minimum-bid prices.

Northrop also has consolidated sales so that fewer districts will be involved. Customs regulations once required that seized or abandoned good be sold by the customhouse that acquired them. But in 1985 those regulations were changed to allow the consolidation of sales, on the theory that if fewer Customs districts were involved, more buyers would show up, competition would heat up, and Customs would get higher prices for its merchandise. Customs also felt that certain merchandise, such as collector-quality firearms and rare birds, which appeal to specific kinds of buyers, would bring a higher price if they could be sold in a district with a concentration of those buyers.

Northrop set up two major centers on either coast, one each in Los Angeles and Newark, New Jersey, to function as centralized sales offices. In 1988, the two central offices began to hold auctions on a regular basis, about every six weeks. Other major customhouses, such as those in Boston, Miami, or San Diego, still hold their own auctions, but these auctions are less frequent. The reorganization of sales applies only to general-order merchandise, however; smuggled goods still are sold in the districts where they're confiscated.

Northrop advertises Customs auctions about a month before they're held. Catalogs of sale items are available at the auction site, and inspection times are usually scheduled a day or so before a sale so that buyers can see the merchandise. Potential buyers are not, however, allowed to touch goods, in order to ensure against damage and pilfering. On the day of the sale, changes in items may be posted outside the auction site.

Customs merchandise is sold by auction or sealed bid. Sealed bids are solicited for some of the larger items, such as cars, and for the property sold in the occasional real estate sales. To participate in sealed bids on cars, you normally have to include a deposit equal to 20 percent of your bid. Bidding at auctions is conducted with numbered paddles. To obtain a paddle and participate in an auction, you have to put down a refundable deposit—usually $20 to $50—and fill in a registration card. In open vehicle auctions, successful bidders usually have to make a deposit on their merchandise immediately after they are declared the winner, with full payment due at the conclusion of the auction. Payment in full is usually required on vehicles bought for $1,000 and under; deposits of $1,000 are normally required on vehicles bought for an amount up to $5,000; and deposits of $2,000 are usual for vehicles bought for amounts from $5,000 to $10,000.

Minimum bids are usually suggested in the auction catalog. They're based on the assessed value of items as determined by professional appraisers. These minimum bids are not necessarily firm, however, and in open auctions it's wise to remain silent to see if the auctioneer will drop the price before you jump in to start the contest.

Articles marked Export Only are sold for exportation only and are not allowed to remain in the United States, although special conditions may apply if the buyer wishes to adapt the merchandise to satisfy U.S. import requirements. For example, certain high-power cordless telephones may be sold abroad, but not in the U.S. Motorcycles that don't meet U.S. safety standards also fit into this category. These conditions usually will be mentioned in the catalog. Any transportation or exportation costs for all merchandise must be borne by the purchaser. A purchaser does not have to pay customs duties on the merchandise but may have to pay delivery and handling charges levied by the warehouse where it's stored.

Northrop will accept MasterCard and Visa credit cards for payment of goods. That innovation was instituted in 1988, after Customs successfully tested a plan for accepting credit cards in payment of duties at several major airports around the country. Payment for auction goods is also accepted in the form of cash, cashier's check, or bank wire, but not personal checks. Payment for merchandise must be made prior to pick-up, which must take place within twenty-four to forty-eight hours. If you don't pick up your goods within the time limit, you forfeit them. You can arrange with the warehouse to keep your merchandise after you pay for it, but it will be stored at your expense. Northrop provides no guarantees or warranties. Sales are final, and no refunds are made.

In order to bid on Customs merchandise, you have to be over eighteen years old and not a Northrop employee or immediate member of an employee's household. Nor can you be a member of the U.S. military or any government agency whose regulations prohibit participation in such sales.

HOW TO FIND OUT ABOUT CUSTOMS SALES

Northrop advertises Customs sales through a subscription service. You can either request a subscription for announcements covering the entire United States, or you can take a subscription for one of two regions, East or West. The East Region covers all states and customs districts located east of the Mississippi River, including Puerto Rico. The

West Region covers all states and territories west of the Mississippi. If you subscribe to the national service, you'll usually receive two to three notices of sales per week.

The price for the national subscription is $30 per year; for each of the regional subscriptions, $15 per year. All subscriptions must be paid with a U.S. Postal Money Order.

For an application to subscribe, write: Northrop Worldwide Aircraft Services, U.S. Customs Service Support Division, P.O. Box 1167, Lawton, OK 73502-1167.

Or call the San Francisco headquarters office at (405) 357-9194.

5

FEDERAL AND LOCAL LAW-
ENFORCEMENT AGENCY SALES

If the TV viewing habits of the general public are any
guide, then it is safe to say the United States has an ongoing
fascination with the drama of police work. Popular television
shows such as *Miami Vice* and *Hill Street Blues* entertain
millions of viewers by showing how tough, streetwise cops
apply the tricks of their trade to bust crime rings and track
down notorious bad guys. But after an arrest is made and the
case brought to a happy conclusion, the credits always roll
before you are shown what happens to the wonderfully
valuable merchandise the police managed to recover. A
question rarely asked, but one worth pondering, is: What
happens to the goodies?

If your answer is that the police return whatever stolen
property they recover to its rightful owner, then you are only
partially correct. The reality is that police work is never as
tidy as it appears on TV—with a well-defined crime and a

well-known victim. More often than not, the proper owners cannot be found.

A recent real-life case that took place in Miami is illustrative. The local police received a tip from an anonymous source that the occupants of a Dade County residence were using their house to fence stolen clothes. In the investigation that followed, an undercover cop walked into the house and paid $140 for a European-tailored suit that normally carried a retail price of $700. After hearing a description of the transactions taking place inside the house, a police lieutenant grimly concluded, "It was a clothing store disguised as a house." The police staged a raid, and, much as they had anticipated, they discovered more than $750,000 worth of stolen suits, dresses, shirts, ties, and other apparel.

After the arrests were made, a bus was brought in to haul the confiscated goods away. But the efforts of the police to locate the rightful owners of the stolen merchandise proved to be perplexing at best. The two men who ran the fencing operation had no idea where the burglars who supplied them with stolen goods had gotten the merchandise, and the burglars remained at large. The routine examination of local crime reports by the police failed to turn up accurate descriptions of the property taken into custody, and all the police could conclude was that most of the merchandise was stolen outside their jurisdiction.

Such an occurrence is far from rare. A similar case took place in Seattle, Washington, where, after a successful sting operation, the police department found that it had literally hundreds upon hundreds of personal computers in its inventory of recovered merchandise, with little or no potential for finding the proper owners. They had Apple, Compaq, and IBM computers sitting in crates and boxes that had never been opened—machines worth thousands of dollars on the open market.

So what do the police do? The answer depends on which enforcement agency, and which level of government, was involved in the enforcement action.

U.S. MARSHALS SERVICE SALES

The U.S. Marshals Service handles disposal of all Justice Department seizures, including those of the Drug Enforcement Administration (DEA) and the Immigration and Naturalization Service's U.S. Border Patrol. Until recently, Justice handed over much of the loot it confiscated from seizures to the GSA for disposal. But the GSA finally decided the headaches involved in sorting out the murky liens on property seized from criminals posed too many headaches, so property involved in Justice Department drug seizures in particular is now disposed of by the U.S. Marshals Service.

George Washington appointed the first thirteen U.S. Marshals under the first Judiciary Act of September 24, 1799. Today, the service has 94 federal marshals and approximately 1,700 deputies posted at regional offices throughout the country. They are the federal government's "policemen," as officers of the federal courts and as enforcers of federal security programs.

Marshals are charged with protecting witnesses to organized crime; providing physical security in U.S. courtrooms and personal protection for federal judges, jurors, and attorneys; carrying out arrests under federal court-ordered warrants; and maintaining the custody of federal prisoners and evidence, including money and property seized pursuant to federal crimes. They also disburse appropriated funds to satisfy government obligations incurred in the administration of justice at the federal level. It is under these last-mentioned responsibilities that the U.S. Marshals Service is empowered to organize the disposal of goods seized and forfeited in conjunction with crime.

The money made from sales of goods seized from criminals goes into the National Asset Massive Seizure of Forfeiture Fund, a general fund maintained by the federal government, which goes back into law-enforcement efforts. The proceeds in the fund are divvied up among federal and local law-enforcement agencies according to the percentage of their participation in individual seizures.

Types of items available. Items sold by the U.S. Marshals Service, along with those sold by U.S. Customs, are among the best of the government's auction lot. They include a preponderance of luxury goods that run the gamut from precious jewelry to fancy mansions. It's said that the best cars are those confiscated by the Drug Enforcement Administration.

Among the more interesting items sold by the U.S. Marshals Service in recent years was a vintage 1943 World War II PBY Seaplane bomber that belonged to a drug dealer. It went in a California auction for $750,000.

Another was a vintage 1963 Ferrari, of which only thirty-two exist in the world. It too belonged to a drug dealer, and it was seized by the service when the dealer fled the country shortly before his body turned up in the countryside of Spain. The Ferrari was sold in Hartford, Connecticut, in 1987 for $1.5 million.

How items get on the U.S. Marshals auction block. Goods seized by the U.S. Marshals Service under the Organized Crime Control Act of 1984 are held in custody by the U.S. Marshal's office involved until their forfeiture is determined by a federal court. That can take months, and sometimes several years.

Once cleared for disposal, seized goods are turned over to local professional auction houses for disposal.

How to find out about U.S. Marshals auctions. Each local U.S. Marshals office manages the disposal of its own goods, so the service maintains no central bidders list. You have to watch your local papers for advertisements of impending sales.

Where to find U.S. Marshals. To find your local U.S. Marshals office, check your yellow pages under Federal Government, or contact the head office at the following address:

U.S. Marshals Service
Department of Justice
One Tysons Corner Center
McLean, VA 22102
(703) 285-1131

LOCAL POLICE AUCTIONS

In most cities, local police departments hold recovered goods for a certain length of time with the hope that the owner will eventually file a claim and produce documentation of ownership. But when this fails to happen, the police liquidate their stockpile of stolen merchandise by conducting public auctions. In fact, no matter where you live, you can rest assured that your local police department or sheriff's department is in possession of an accumulation of valuable merchandise that they need to dispose of, and that they will make available to the highest bidder. Because the police are more interested in getting rid of these goods quickly than they are in making money, these auctions always provide fantastic buys.

Items available at police and sheriff auctions. What are you likely to find at a local police-department or sheriff's auction? First of all, you're bound to find a wide range of merchandise that is attractive to thieves. Small items that are easy to conceal, such as decorative jewelry, cameras, tape recorders, and wristwatches, are always in evidence, as are automobiles, motorcycles, mopeds, and bicycles, which are among the most commonly reported thefts in every city of the United States. The items sold at a recent police-department auction in Washington, D.C., for example, included a white Mercedes-Benz, a 25-piece set of sterling-silver cutlery, an antique silver hairbrush, hundreds of clocks, long racks of clothes, and thousands of television sets, stereos, calculators, gold chains, bracelets, and rings.

Much of this merchandise is brand new and, like the computers in Seattle, can be found in freshly opened boxes. Virtually all of the retail merchandise recovered by the police is in excellent condition. In addition, however, the police accumulate a lot of used junk that has been pilfered from homes, schools, and businesses and is then left sitting in a dusty storage room for years on end. Therefore it is important to approach police auctions with a selective eye and carefully examine all of the items that interest you during the viewing period.

In addition to unclaimed stolen goods, police departments also auction off valuable lost personal property—such as a camera or a leather briefcase accidentally left behind on a city bus or in a public restroom. When such goods are turned over to the police, they are stored in lost and found for a set period of time, usually ranging from sixty days to six months. Then, if the item is still unclaimed and the police department determines that it has a resale value of $10 or more, that item is included in the auction collection. If it is valued at less than $10, then it is destroyed.

Quite naturally, the police confiscate a large number of guns and knives. In years past, numerous police and sheriff's departments included handguns and rifles in their auction collections. But this practice is less common now. "We melt down all our guns and knives," explained the property division clerk in Alexandria, Virginia. "We burn drugs and destroy alcohol. Other than that, we'll sell almost anything that is of reasonable value." While many jurisdictions melt down guns, there are some jurisdictions that continue to auction them. Due to registration laws, guns are usually sold at special auctions where the buyer must submit to a security check and wait for three to five days to claim the merchandise.

How police auctions work. The procedures that govern how local police and sheriff's departments conduct their auctions vary from city to city, and jurisdiction to jurisdiction. In large cities, the auctions are often two-day affairs, with general merchandise sold on one day and motor vehicles sold the next. Police departments in most major cities conduct their auctions on a periodic basis, holding anywhere from one to ten auctions per year. Rather than setting a fixed schedule, the police tend to have public sales as the need arises. Entry fees of $2 to $5 are not uncommon and are used to defray the cost of holding the auction.

In some communities, rather than conducting the auction themselves, the police contract with a local auction company to conduct the sales. The auction company obtains its profit by claiming a percentage of gross receipts.

This has both advantages and disadvantages for the buyer. The fact that a professional auctioneer is responsible for the sale usually guarantees that the auction proceedings will be smooth and efficient. The viewing period will take place in a well-appointed room, and you won't have to go poking through old boxes stuck in a dark corner of a basement store-room. However, it is also likely that a professional auctioneer will have a much better feel for the *value* of the goods being sold. This is particularly true for items such as antique jewelry, silver, and crystal, which can slip past an inexperienced po-liceman's eye without so much as a blink. One of the great advantages of shopping at police auctions is that antique jew-elry is often lumped together with tawdry costume jewelry, and a knowledgeable connoisseur can make a fantastic killing. But professional auctioneers are much more likely to make people aware of any valuable antiques in their possession and will often advertise them in public notices prior to the sale. The end result is that bidding on such items is likely to begin at a much higher price and be much more competitive.

Tips for shopping at police auctions. The most important opportunity you have at any auction comes during the viewing period, when you are allowed to inspect the goods being put on the block. Local police departments are always eager to get rid of their unclaimed goods with as little bother as possible, and the viewing time at police auctions is notoriously short. It is not uncommon for police departments to limit viewing to the hour that precedes the sale. So it is extremely important to make the most of the limited time available.

In order to make the viewing period work to your advantage, it is suggested that you make a standard practice of the following:

• Bring a notepad and pencil to the viewing period. Once the bidding begins, things move quickly. Merchandise is often sold by lot number, but the police do not necessarily proceed in order, and it is easy to become confused. "I always advise people to jot down the lot number of the items that interest them, and to make notes," said one police auctioneer. The notes you make during the viewing period become your most important guide once the action begins.

• Bring a flashlight to the public inspection. Police auctions are frequently held in the warehouse where the goods have been stored, or in the basement of a county courthouse. Merchandise is dumped in cardboard boxes and shoved into dark corners, where a flashlight will help in determining the condition of some of the items you examine.

• If you are shopping for antiques or jewelry, bring a magnifying glass. Costume jewelry is often lumped together with expensive items, and it is important to look carefully. It is also wise to keep an up-to-date price guide on hand so you can check the current value of items that interest you.

• Determine the maximum amount you are willing to spend on an item prior to the auction, write that figure down in your notebook, and stick to it. Remember that an auctioneer's job is to extract every possible penny from the crowd. You should never exceed your preset limit in response to something an auctioneer says, or allow yourself to get caught up in the bidding fever that frequently occurs at auctions.

• Come with cash. Most police departments do not accept personal checks or credit cards. Payment in cash is expected upon acceptance of the winning bid.

Buying a car at a police auction. Abandoned vehicles and property confiscated because it was used in the commission of a crime can also be found in police auction inventories. This practice guarantees that a large number of automobiles and vans will be auctioned off by local police departments every year.

Buying a used car at a police auction is nothing like buying a car off a dealer's lot. In fact, it can be an extraordinary adventure, as an unsuspecting buyer in Seattle discovered when he was arrested four days after purchasing a Vega station wagon for $65 at a police auction. The charge? Possession of a stolen vehicle. It seems that the car was stolen and then seized by police in a drug raid. At the time of the theft, the original owner was unable to provide the police with a vehicle identification number, and after recovery of the car they never returned the car to its rightful owner. When he received his registration renewal notice in the mail, he filed a new report that contained the proper identification number. The police then placed the car on their stolen vehicles list, which was circulated a couple of days after the police had conducted their auction. Later that week, when the new buyer was stopped for a minor traffic violation, he was dismayed to find himself being carted off to jail. While such an occurrence is rare, it does serve to underscore the point that buying a car at a police auction may be a risky business. Protect yourself by keeping your auction receipt!

You usually don't run the risk of an unexpected arrest, but you should be aware of the fact that the way in which the police come into possession of the motor vehicles they sell guarantees that a large number of the cars they put on the block will be suffering from mechanical and maintenance problems. Police obtain cars, trucks, and vans in a variety of ways. Many vehicles that come into the hands of the police are abandoned vehicles that have simply been left on the street and are eventually hauled off to a police storage lot. Police departments are also responsible for towing illegally parked cars, and occasionally the owner never arrives to claim the car. (This may be due to a large backlog of unpaid parking tickets, or an outstanding arrest warrant that makes it unwise for the owner to come in contact with the police.) When the owner fails to appear, the car in question is included in the lot of vehicles being made available for public sale. Local law-enforcement agencies also have the authority to confiscate vehicles that have been used in the commission of a crime, such as drug dealing or armed robbery, when the car is used to depart from the scene of the crime.

What does this mean for the buyer? The commander of the property division of the New York Police Department is careful to warn prospective auction attendees, "We don't advise anyone to buy anything without looking at it." But look is all you can do. Test drives are not permitted. No matter what condition the car is in, you can rest assured it has been sitting in an outdoor lot for a long, long time—frequently for as much as a year or two, or even longer. During the viewing period, it is not uncommon to see cars with flat tires or missing batteries. Many have been corroded by rust. In the case of vehicles that have been towed, ignition keys are usually not available, and the first thing you have to do after making your purchase is visit a locksmith. In New York, one officer explained that people often come expecting to find souped-up cars that have been seized from pimps, drug dealers, and syndicate kingpins. "Unfortunately," he said, "too many people watch TV and expect that's the way life is. We're in the business of realities." And the reality is that most abandoned and unclaimed cars are not worth much.

Still, one should not despair. While a lot of junk is on

display, good buys can be found, and with a little bit of work the careful shopper can obtain a serviceable car for a small amount of money. And every once in a while—much to everyone's delight—that rare Mercedes-Benz or Jaguar is put on the block.

Experts familiar with police car auctions offer a number of tips to help you assess the value of the cars being sold. First, keep a car-price book handy as a reference guide during the viewing period, and check prices at a used-car dealer prior to attending the auction. Check to see if the car is carrying any optional equipment that will increase its value, such as an automatic transmission, air conditioning, or a tape player. Examine the tires and upholstery. The condition of the interior provides the best clue as to how well the car has been maintained. If possible, start the engine to see how well it runs. Look for rust on the chassis and in the wheel wells. Finally, on cars that have an automatic transmission, check the transmission fluid. If the fluid is black rather than pink, then it is likely that the car has transmission problems.

Who attends police car auctions and how competitive are they? Used-car dealers and junkyard operators buying for parts are regular attendees, and their presence guarantees that the bidding will be reasonably competitive. But since they are out to make a profit, they cut their bids well below blue-book value, which leaves plenty of room for the individual buyer to come away with a good deal. If you find something you like at a police auction, the odds are that you'll come away much more cheaply than if you were to buy a similar car off of a used-car lot.

How to find out about police auctions. The best way to find out about police and sheriff's auctions is to call your local police or sheriff's department, and ask for the property division. They will be able to tell you how often auctions are conducted, and if any are scheduled for the near future. Most police departments do not maintain mailing lists, although it never hurts to ask. As we move further and further into the computer age, mailing lists are less cumbersome to maintain and are a bit more common than in the past. As was mentioned earlier, some police departments do not conduct public sales themselves but sell the rights to do so to an auction company. At the very least, the property division will be able to tell you how it disposes of unclaimed merchandise. If they do not do it themselves, they can give you the name of the private auction house or law-enforcement agency that handles the sale.

While public notification procedures vary from jurisdiction to jurisdiction, almost all police and sheriff's departments advertise in local newspapers the week of the sale. Your best bet is to make a habit of checking the auction notices in the classified section of your newspaper every Thursday and Friday. Most police auctions are held on the weekend, and Thursday and Friday are the days the auction notices are most likely to run.

Quite often, police-department notices are among the most informative you will ever find. In order to give the rightful owners of unclaimed merchandise one last chance to claim their property, the police department's public notice will list every item they intend to put on the block. If the owner sees his or her property listed and can produce proof of ownership, then that item will be returned to the owner provided that the claim is made prior to the day of the sale.

But the system doesn't always work perfectly. In 1987, Pam and Jay Knox, of Washington, D.C., were looking forward to getting back their jewelry, VCR, and camera. The Washington police, who had recovered their property in 1984, had been holding on to it as evidence in a case against a burglar who had robbed forty-four homes from May to July 1984. By accident, after the trial the police sold the Knoxes' and ten other families' possessions. Now the D.C. police, as well as other police departments, use computers to keep track of property that might end up on the auction block.

6

DEPARTMENT OF DEFENSE SALES

The Department of Defense (DOD) sells enormous amounts of surplus personal property in over 1,700 sales per year held at hundreds of military installations around the United States and overseas. In recent years, the DOD's annual sales have averaged about $100 million. Most of the DOD's merchandise, however, is of interest primarily to industries or small businesses. And the majority of it is well worn.

Primary responsibility for the DOD's surplus-property sales program belongs to the Defense Reutilization and Marketing Service (DRMS). DRMS is a division of the Defense Logistics Agency (DLA), a joint-services agency of the DOD that handles supply and disposal of property for all the branches of the military. Almost every U.S. military base in the world has a DLA office.

TYPES OF ITEMS AVAILABLE

The DOD sells primarily personal property, although, as one DLA officer says, there's nothing very personal about most of it. Sales of military real property are handled primarily by the General Services Administration.

The DOD's surplus is abundant, divided into over seventy major categories and almost five hundred subcategories (as you might expect from the Pentagon). But although some of it is consumer-type goods, most of it is pretty unexciting stuff—unless you're looking for industrial or business equipment or supplies. Even the occasional "exciting" stuff is hard to find, as the DOD doesn't market its goods the way other government agencies do. Several years ago the duplicate of the "moon vehicle," which was used to train *Apollo I* astronauts for their historic landing on the moon, was sold without fanfare in a Florida auction as just another piece of government surplus. It wasn't until after the sale, when someone just happened to notice the fine print in the catalog description, that the identity of the strange vehicle was brought to the attention of the press.

One of the few "choice" auction items that DLA officials can readily recall is the presidential yacht *Sequoia,* which was disposed of on orders from President Jimmy Carter during his administration. The 110-foot teakwood boat, with a history that went back past Franklin Roosevelt, had been beautifully maintained down through the years by the Navy. But President Carter found no use for it and decided it was a luxury the federal government couldn't afford. It was sold for about $225,000 to a private foundation, which donated it back to the Navy for display to the public. The Navy still hasn't found a way to put the yacht to use, however, and it remains in storage in Maryland.

DOD surplus falls under one of two headings, either recyclable materials or usable property. Recyclable materials include all kinds of waste items—such as paper, metal, or food wastes—that are deemed to have reached the end of their usefulness as is. Usable property is everything else that still has some use left in it, even if only for scrap.

The range of merchandise is wide; it includes the military-type items you may—or may *not*—expect, such as used guided-missile launchers, airplanes, boats, and air-force fighter helmets, as well as such not-so-typical military items as musical instruments, household furniture, and clothing. The DOD even sells live animals.

"Combat" property, such as weapons, ammunition, fighter jets, warships, and armored vehicles, are not sold in original form to the general public. Such items are either "demilitarized" or reduced to recyclable materials before they're auctioned. Demilitarization means melting, scrapping, or cutting an item in such a way that it can't be used in its original form any longer. Demilitarization normally leaves items with no value except for that of their basic material content, or as a display item. If you'd like a cannon for your backyard, this may be the way to acquire one.

Once in a while, though, some of the combat items do get sold to the public by accident. In one such instance, two dozen armed rockets were sold in 1987 to a Mexican businessman at Fort Bliss, near El Paso, Texas. The businessman was in the habit of buying empty wooden crates from the base to stock his lumberyard in Juarez, just across the border. The rockets were packed in crates, which had been inadvertently placed among the empties on sale as surplus. Fort Bliss personnel came across one of the boxed rockets—the only one left behind—after the businessman had removed his purchase. They realized what had happened and immediately notified the Mexican police, who quickly recovered the rest.

The DOD also sells contractor inventory, which is government-owned property that was acquired by, or is in the possession of, a contractor or subcontractor that didn't need it to complete the project. You can find out about what's available by writing one of the addresses listed at the end of this chapter.

Vehicles. If you're looking for a cheap car, a DOD auction is the place to find one. Like the government's other auctioneers, the DOD sets a minimum price it will accept for its merchandise, yet by the time the DOD's vehicles hit the auction block, their fair market value is relatively low. More than any other branch of the government, the DOD gets its money's worth out of the cars it buys. The only vehicles without high mileage are those that have been in accidents. The DOD has no set turnover cycle for acquisitions but drives its vehicles until their maintenance is no longer cost-effective, usually about five to seven years after purchase. The DOD attempts to sell its cars for a return within the range of 5 to 15 percent of the original cost. (And remember, the government buys wholesale.) Normally, the agency sets minimum bids that will allow it to get about a 7-percent return. For instance, on a car that originally cost the DOD $6,000, the minimum bid would be about $420.

The DOD has the full range of car brands and models you'll find at GSA sales, although their colors will almost always be black, dark-blue, or gray. And the DOD has no fancy confiscated cars like Customs or the Marshals Service.

Its vehicles all are "work" vehicles. Many of them must be demilitarized before being sold to the public.

While you might think the DOD would be a good place to buy a Jeep, in fact, the agency sells few Jeeps suitable for driving. The DOD occasionally sells a limited number of M-38 series Jeeps in working order and suitable for public highway use. However, the majority of the DOD's Jeep inventory consist of those in the M-151 series, which have been determined unsafe for public highway use by the National Highway Traffic Safety Administration. As a result, most are sold only for scrap; they're crushed or cut up before they can be taken away by a buyer.

Among the more interesting vehicles sold by the DOD are the tow tractors used to guide airplanes to takeoff and parking spots on air fields. Buyers have fixed some of these up and converted them into golf carts.

The military's warships, battleships, cruisers, frigates, submarines, and other multiton craft, including combat aircraft, are sold for scrapping purposes only. Before being sold, these items are cut in such a manner that they have no value except for basic material content. The DOD also has a number of noncombat ships and boats—such as tugboats—that it does sell as is, in working order. Sales of all ships are organized by the DRMR office in Columbus, Ohio.

HOW DOD AUCTIONS WORK

Department of Defense surplus is sold by auction, sealed bid, spot bid, or negotiation. Small quantities of certain items also are sold at some military installations as regular retail merchandise, at prices based on their current market value.

The Defense Reutilization and Marketing Service conducts a national on-site auction when a substantial quantity or variety of property with wide commercial application is being offered for sale. Local auctions are conducted when there is a wide variety of small quantities of property.

Sealed-bid sales are used to dispose of large quantities of property through regional or national marketing. Recyclable materials almost always are sold this way. Prospective buyers write their bids on a bid form contained in the catalog sent to everyone on the National Bidders List, then return it with a deposit. All bids are opened on a specified day, and all bidders are notified by mail about the outcome.

The DRMS sells surplus through spot bids when there is a variety of property of substantial interest in demand in a local market. Spot bids are conducted much like auctions, and bidders must be present to participate. Prospective buyers must submit their bids on forms provided by the local office. You have to get your name on a local mailing list for these sales.

Negotiated sales are sometimes organized by the DRMS if acceptable bids have not been offered after public advertising, or when it is better for public health or safety to get rid of property in an expedient manner. An example might be gunpowder, because of its potential to harm. Another might be hospital equipment, because of a public need. Negotiated sales usually involve property sold to states, local governments, or tax-supported agencies.

All property for sale by the DOD is described in catalogs in exhaustive detail—often to the point of tediousness. The DOD guarantees the accuracy of its descriptions. However, you are urged to inspect the items you may be interested in, if possible. If you find an error in a description after you've made a purchase, the DRMS, unlike other government agencies, may refund your money or make any necessary changes in the merchandise.

Sealed bids must be accompanied by a deposit, normally 20 percent of your bid. The DRMS has devised a system of accepting "bid-deposit bonds" from frequent bidders, which enable them to make a "permanent" deposit with their local DRMS office so they won't have to make a separate deposit with each bid. The minimum bid-deposit bond usually is $500. Two types are available: Deposit Bond-Individual Invitation, Sale of Government Personal Property (Standard Form 150); and Deposit Bond-Annual, Sale of Government Personal Property (Standard Form 151). You may obtain these forms and instructions from the main headquarters of the DRMS in Battle Creek, Michigan.

Successful bidders may not remove property from the DOD sales site until they've made full payment within the time limit specified. DRMS sales representatives will provide you with a list of common carriers and packing firms if you need help in getting your purchase to its destination. It does not, however, recommend specific carriers, nor will it make the arrangements for you.

After each national sale, the DRMS prepares a list of the successful bidders and the prices they paid for each item. If you'd like a copy of one of these lists, you may obtain it from the local sales office that conducted the sale.

HOW TO FIND OUT ABOUT DOD AUCTIONS

The DOD's Defense Reutilization and Marketing Service conducts both local and national sales, which are advertised in the *Commerce Business Daily* and to subscribers on its National Bidders List. Separate bidders lists are maintained by each local office and by DRMR-Europe, which conducts sales of DOD surplus property located overseas. You have to write to each of these offices separately to get on their lists.

When you apply to be added to a mailing list, the DRMS will send you a pamphlet titled "How to Buy Surplus Personal Property from the United States Department of Defense." The pamphlet contains an application form for the National Bidders List, which must be returned to the DRMS's headquarters. On the application form, you must check off the categories of merchandise and regional sales areas in which you're interested.

When filling out your application for the national list or one of the local lists, you must be careful to fill in your *entire* zip code, including the four-digit extension. The DOD is rather sticky about this detail and won't add your name to the list if you don't supply a nine-digit zip code. If you don't know the extension of your zip code, just ask your local post office.

Once your name is entered on the DOD's National Bidders List, you will receive a pamphlet titled "Sale by Reference," which includes instructions, terms, and conditions of DOD sales. Keep this pamphlet for reference. It also will have your own permanent individual bidder's number in the upper right-hand corner of the mailing label. You cannot bid on items unless you use this bidder's number.

If you fail to make a bid after five mailings of sale announcements from the national list, your name will be purged, unless you write to request that it remain on the list. For the local lists, your name will be purged after only two mailings.

DLA Offices Providing Info
on DOD Contractor Inventory

Commander, DLA
Defense Contract Administration Services Region, **Atlanta**
805 Walker Street
Marietta, GA 30060-2789

Commander, DLA
Defense Contract Administration Services Region, **Boston**
495 Summer Street
Boston, MA 02210-2184

Commander, DLA
Defense Contract Administration Services Region, **Chicago**
O'Hare International Airport
P.O. Box 66475
Chicago, IL 60666-0475

Commander, DLA
Defense Contract Administration Services Region,
Cleveland
Federal Office Building
1240 E. Ninth Street
Cleveland, OH 44199-2036

Commander, DLA
Defense Contract Administration Services Region, **Dallas**
1200 Main Street
Dallas, TX 75202-4399

Commander, DLA
Defense Contract Administration Services Region,

Los Angeles
11099 South La Cienega Boulevard
Los Angeles, CA 90045-6197

Commander, DLA
Defense Contract Administration Services Region,
New York
201 Varick Street
New York, NY 10014-4811

Commander, DLA
Defense Contract Administration Services Region,
Philadelphia
2800 S. 20th Street
Philadelphia, PA 19101-7478

Commander, DLA
Defense Contract Administration Services Region, **St. Louis**
1136 Washington Avenue
St. Louis, MO 63101-1194

Defense Reutilization and Marketing Service (DRMS) Regional Sales Offices

To get your name on the **National Bidders List,** write the DRMS's headquarters at the following address:

DOD Bidders Control Office
P.O. Box 1370
Battle Creek, MI 49016-1370
(616) 961-7331 or 7332

To get your name on the **European mailing list** or one of the **local mailing lists,** write to the appropriate address below.

DRMR Region Columbus
P.O. Box 500
Blacklick, OH 43004-0500
(614) 238-2114

DRMR Region Memphis
P.O. 14716
Memphis, TN 38114-0716
(901) 775-6417

DRMR Region Ogden
P.O. Box 53
Defense Depot Ogden
Ogden, UT 84407-5001
(801) 399-7257

DRMR Region Europe
APO NY 09633
Phone: 06212-82-3505

Buyers located outside the United States should contact the following addresses:

DRMR-Europe
Postfach 2027
D6200 Wiesbaden
West Germany

DRMR Sales Office Hawaii
Box 211
Pearl City, HI 96782-0211
(808) 455-5158

DRMR Australia
FPO San Francisco 96680-2920
Phone: 099-49-3214

Buyers located outside the United States should use the following address:

U.S. Naval Communications Station
Exmouth, Western Australia

DRMR Canadian Sales Office
Crown Assets Disposal Corporation
P.O. Box 8451
Ottawa, Ontario
Canada K1G3J8
(819) 994-0074

Part 3

BUYING REAL ESTATE
FROM THE GOVERNMENT

7

HOW THE GOVERNMENT
OBTAINS AUCTIONABLE REAL ESTATE

Are you in the market for a beautiful home? Some lakefront vacation property? A small real estate investment? A business development site? If your answer to any of the above is yes, then it would be well worth your while to explore government-sponsored real estate auctions.

Selling real estate through auction is fast, clean, and efficient. It is not uncommon for a real estate agent to take several weeks or months to move a single piece of property, showing it over and over again before a deal is completed. But local, state, and federal government agencies all want to move property as quickly as possible, and an auction is the most expedient method for doing so. These days, it seems, everybody is getting into the act, and in 1987 alone more than 100,000 real estate transactions were undertaken by a wide variety of government agencies.

The properties that have been put on the government

auction block in the not-too-distant past include: the ice rink where the United States Olympic hockey team won a gold medal in 1980; a ten-acre plot of harbor land near the Brooklyn-Queens border valued at more than $13 million; several elegant Florida estates that once belonged to multimillion-dollar narcotics kingpins; the Hollywood Hills home of jazz great Woody Herman; the private residence of convicted spy John Walker; and thousands upon thousands of ordinary homes, lots, abandoned buildings, vacation sites, and business dwellings. In fact, the only thing that such a diverse range of private property has in common is that it is all available to the highest bidder.

Who is responsible for conducting these sales? The answer varies according to how the property was acquired and the reason for the sale. Several agencies within the federal government conduct real-property sales on a periodic basis. These include the General Services Agency, the Internal Revenue Service, the United States Marshals Service, the Department of the Interior, and the Department of Agriculture, to name a few. In addition, local law-enforcement agencies, state government agencies, and city and country governments are also responsible for the sale of vast tracts of land every year.

Government agencies at both the local and federal level acquire real property in a variety of ways, and what you find on sale at a public auction is usually obtained through one of four different methods. Far and away the most common is the seizure of property as a consequence of a delinquent tax debt. Just as the Internal Revenue Service generates most of its revenue through direct taxation of individuals and businesses, most cities and municipalities are equally dependent upon direct taxation to obtain their operating revenue. Unlike the IRS, however, local governments levy property taxes on individual residences, businesses, and vacant plots of land. When those taxes go unpaid, city governments possess the authority to seize the property, and this is how local governments obtain the vast majority of the real estate they put up for auction. The IRS does not levy property taxes, but it does have the authority to seize private property to liquidate delinquent tax claims and is also involved in real estate acquisition due to tax debt.

The statutes involved in real estate acquisition determine which agency of the government is responsible for initiating any necessary seizure proceedings at both the national and local levels, and this, in turn, determines which governmental department will handle the disposition of the sale. In general terms, local governments tend to be much more active in real estate seizures than the federal government, and it is at the local level that interested buyers will find the largest amount of real estate turnover.

A second way in which government agencies come into possession of auction property is by seizing real estate that was purchased through ill-gotten gains. Prior to the late 1970s this was rarely done, but in the move to get tough on drug traffickers, property seizure has become a favorite weapon of law-enforcement authorities. The past decade has seen more and more state governments, as well as the federal government, turning to statutes that hit criminals where it really hurts—in their pocketbooks. Nationwide, drug-related real estate seizures now total over $100 million annually, and because of the success that law-enforcement authorities have encountered, the Department of Justice recently expanded the size of its manpower force working on criminal property foreclosures.

These property seizures, however, are by no means restricted to crimes involving drug smuggling. If a piece of property was purchased with income derived from illegal activity, then the government has the right to seize that property and auction it off to the highest bidder.

In the farm belt, one of the most common reasons for initiating foreclosure has nothing to do with criminal activity but results from the state of the economy. When times are bad for farmers, it is inevitable that federally guaranteed loans will slip into default. When the loan cannot be redeemed, the federal government has no option other than to lay claim to the family farm. Of course, government-sponsored loans are not limited to farmers but also include small-business loans, urban-redevelopment initiatives, and low-income housing projects, in addition to numerous other government-sponsored activities. When the loans underwritten to initiate private-sector involvement in these programs go bad, the government often finds itself in possession of valuable real estate that it is eager to return to the private sector. And it does so by public auction.

Finally, the government is always in possession of property that it no longer deems useful. This happened not too long ago when the United States Navy closed a small base in Key West, Florida. The base had been a favorite vacation retreat for Harry Truman during his presidency, and the news of its sale in 1986 stirred worldwide interest. On the auction block, the 102-acre parcel of land brought the federal government more than $17 million in revenue and put an end to the expenses incurred by the Navy for maintaining the site. On a less spectacular level, whenever a post office closes its doors or a government warehouse is shut down, the government must decide what to do with the property. Frequently, the government wants nothing other than to get rid of it, which can provide great opportunities to individuals in search of real estate bargains. Post office buildings that have closed and Postal Service land is auctioned by the General Services Administration.

HOW GOVERNMENT REAL ESTATE AUCTIONS WORK

There is no set procedure universally applied to government-sponsored real estate auctions, but virtually all of them take one of two forms: they are either open-bid or sealed-bid auctions. Open-bid auctions are the kind with which most of us are familiar, where an auctioneer stands in front of the bidding audience calling out prices until a winner is declared. At an open-bid auction, every bid must be made in public, and nothing is kept secret from any of the interested parties.

Just the reverse is true in sealed-bid auctions. After public notice is given by the agency conducting the sale, all bids remain secret until *after* the winner is declared. Each bidder is allowed to tender only one bid and must deliver that bid in a sealed envelope. The great advantage of a sealed-bid sale is that it can be conducted by mail, which gives the government an opportunity to expand dramatically the size of the bidding audience on property that is of interest to a wide geographic area. Government agencies frequently turn to sealed-bid sales when they are auctioning off property that has an unusually high market value, or when the property is deemed to be of interest to a narrow buying audience. In such cases, the agency will solicit bids from parties it has reason to believe might be interested in tendering a bid and usually requires that a large deposit be submitted along with the bid.

One feature common to most government-sponsored real estate auctions is that a minimum price on each piece of property to be sold is set prior to the public sale. This is true for both open-bid and closed-bid auctions. Frequently, the minimum acceptable bid is published prior to the auction proceedings or is called out by the auctioneer as the base price at which the bidding is to begin. But there is no obligation that the minimum acceptable bid be made public prior to the sale, and on occasion a high bidder will be informed that his or her bid is unacceptable. The practice of establishing a minimum bid diminishes the likelihood of collusion among interested parties and guarantees that government-owned property will generate at least a reasonable amount of revenue even when the sale price falls well short of market value. If the minimum acceptable bid is not reached, the property remains in possession of the government and is put up for auction at a later date, maintained and administered by the government, or leased out to a private party.

Many agencies within the federal government, such as the General Services Administration and the Internal Revenue Service, are responsible for conducting their own auctions, and they do so according to their own procedures. In years past it has been a routine practice for the General Services Administration to preside over the liquidation of property in the possession of numerous federal departments and agencies. But due to the increase in federal government real estate seizures and transactions, some agencies, such as the Department of Justice and the U.S. Marshals Service, are becoming more active in handling the auctions themselves. With the establishment of property seizure as one of the weapons of choice in the fight against drug trafficking and organized crime, this trend is expected to become even more prevalent in the years ahead.

At the local level, most large cities in the United States maintain control over their real estate auctions. But it is not uncommon for smaller cities and municipalities to hire a professional auctioneer to handle their property sales. The private auctioneer is usually much more skilled at maximizing the amount of money brought in by a residential dwelling or a plot of land than local government officials. Over the years private auctioneers can be expected to develop promotional skills and a body of regular business clients that they can call on to enhance the public interest in the properties being sold. By tapping these resources, private auctioneers frequently increase the competitiveness of government-sponsored auctions. They are also more likely to resort to innovative selling techniques. For example, in recent years private auctioneers engaged in selling off mortgage-foreclosed farmland have turned to the practice of dividing the land into subdivisions. Since the purchase of 3,000 or 4,000 acres of fertile farmland is more than most citizens can afford, dividing it into smaller parcels causes the average per-acre price to rise dramatically, and the number of potential buyers to increase greatly.

TIPS FOR REAL ESTATE BUYERS

You may be curious to know how competitive real estate auctions are and what kind of prices you might expect to find. Of course, there is no perfectly reliable answer, but everyone involved in real estate auctions is quick to testify to the fact that tremendous bargains are out there waiting to be had. In fact, there are a number of self-made millionaires in the United States who have amassed their fortunes by trading in real estate purchased at auction. The trick, no matter how small or large an investment you want to make, is to do your homework. This means that you should always inspect the property you are interested in bidding on and obtain a reliable estimate of its fair market value.

In large cities, the bidding tends to be much more competitive than in rural areas, and in the cities you'll be more likely to find a large number of real estate professionals in the audience hoping to sneak away with some property that will bring a handsome profit on resale. Their presence guarantees that the bidding will be reasonably competitive on attractive lots and residences. However, those lots and dwellings that suffer from poor location or lack of upkeep draw much less of a response and sometimes remain unsold. At the annual property auction in New York City, a huge crowd packs itself into the auction room, and attendees are advised to arrive early in the morning. Latecomers sometimes find that it is impossible to get into the room and place a bid. "Bidding has become much more fierce," says a New York appraiser who has been attending the city-run auctions for thirty years. "Today people like to own their own home. For many, this is the only way."

Prior to attending a government-sponsored real estate auction, you should carefully inspect the properties that interest you. Public inspection is usually permitted a couple of weeks prior to the auction and is done on an "open house" basis. You do not have a tour guide or a real estate agent to take you through the building but are left to wander about at your leisure. Be sure that you carry a flashlight on your inspection rounds, and check for structural damage. Keep in mind that the residences and dwellings seized by governmental authorities have frequently been left standing vacant for prolonged periods of time. When heat and utilities are shut off, pipes can burst, walls can rot, and the house can become infested with rodents or termites. What may sound like a tremendous opportunity on paper often proves to be much less enticing when you are standing in the middle of it. Any structural damage you discover should be taken into account in your determination of the value of the property.

For buildings and residences that are in need of repair, code violations—no matter how minor—must be cured by the purchaser within a reasonable amount of time. Just because the city sold you a home or a building that was in violation of housing standards does not mean that you will be granted a waiver exempting you from the enforcement of local ordinances. On the contrary, all real estate is sold with the explicit understanding that the buyer will assume the responsibility for bringing all property violations into accordance with the law.

Your assessment of property value cannot be complete without an awareness of the rules that govern the auction, as well as a review of the financial history of the property under consideration. At some real estate auctions, all property is sold free and clear of liens, penalties, and back taxes. Other times, however, the sale is only for the rights and title possessed by the previous owner prior to the government seizure. If this is the case, the buyer is expected to satisfy all claims, including outstanding mortgage debts and third-party liens, at the time of purchase. In those auctions where the property is sold free and clear, the situation is relatively straightforward. But when you are purchasing the title rights possessed by the previous owner, your transactions can become extraordinarily complex, and it is imperative to proceed with caution. This is not to suggest that you should avoid sales when the buyer assumes outstanding claims, because tremendous bargains can be found at these sales, but it is to say that you should always be aware of the rules that govern any real estate purchases you are considering.

HOW TO FIND OUT ABOUT
GOVERNMENT-SPONSORED REAL ESTATE AUCTIONS

Happily, it is easy to obtain information about government-sponsored real estate auctions, and you can accumulate a wealth of information without ever leaving the house. Whenever a local government or municipality auctions off a parcel of real estate, it is required by law to advertise in large-circulation newspapers published in the city or county where the auction is to take place. A close examination of real estate auction notices in your local newspaper is an excellent way to keep informed about upcoming local real estate auctions. Additionally, most cities and municipalities with populations in excess of 500,000 maintain mailing lists that they use to send out public notices in advance of the sale. To find out how you can be included on these mailing lists, simply call the property-management division of the local government and inquire about the procedures that apply. Quite often, all it takes is a phone call to get your name on the mailing list. Large cities, such as Chicago, New York, and Los Angeles, also produce brochures that not only list the properties being sold but provide valuable information regarding each property. These brochures can be purchased from the city government for a small fee.

Federal agencies, which operate in a similar fashion, rely primarily on local advertising to get the word out. All federal agencies are required by law to place a public notice in the local newspaper where the auction is being conducted. When the property being sold has an unusually high value, as was the case when the General Services Administration presided over the sale of several Florida estates seized in drug raids, advertisements were also placed in such large-circulation newspapers as the *Wall Street Journal,* the *Christian Science*

Monitor, the *New York Times,* and the *Washington Post.* Federal agencies also maintain a wide range of mailing lists. For example, the Internal Revenue Service is divided into fifty-eight different geographic regions, and each regional office maintains a separate mailing list for the residents residing in or near that particular region, while the General Services Administration maintains a separate mailing list for real-property auctions.

The practice of hiring private auctioneers to preside over government-sponsored auctions has become more common in recent years, and because private auctioneers are in business to make money, they tend to do whatever they can to heighten public interest. Virtually all of them maintain up-to-date mailing lists which they would be happy to place your name on. Therefore an inquiry to your local government regarding any third parties who handle their real estate could provide you with a further source of valuable information.

All in all, a few well-placed telephone calls, coupled with an examination of real estate notices in your local newspaper, will keep you well informed of what is taking place in regard to government-sponsored real estate auctions.

8

GOVERNMENT BUILDINGS AND PROPERTY AVAILABLE FROM THE GENERAL SERVICES ADMINISTRATION

Along with disposing of excess personal property, the General Services Administration is also charged with disposing of federal property and buildings.

Among the more interesting properties to come up for auction was the old U.S. Assay Office, the "Fort Knox of the East Coast," located in the Wall Street area of New York City. An international consortium bid $27 million for the building, which once was used to melt and store gold and other precious metals, and where a chimney sweep once swept up $200,000 of gold dust.

But the majority of the GSA's real estate holdings are a bit more mundane than that. A typical list of holdings published by the GSA in 1988 included a former post office in Suffolk, Virginia; a mobile home and wood-frame barn on ten acres of land in Thurston County, Washington; about twenty acres of unimproved land along the Intercostal Waterway in Gulf Shores, Alabama; a nursing-home complex in Beardstown, Illinois; a portion of the U.S. Coast Guard LORAN Station on the island of Kauai; part of the Niagara Falls International Airport; and a former U.S. Border Patrol station in Eagle Pass, Texas.

The Federal Property and Administrative Services Act of 1949 requires all federal agencies to report their unwanted real estate, except for some exempted categories, to the GSA, either for transfer to another federal agency or for disposal as surplus property. The act exempts public-domain lands, national forests and parks, and certain property where disposal is an integral part of an agency's statutory responsibility. An example of real estate sales that come under the statutory responsibility of an agency and thus are not administered by the GSA would be the Department of Housing and Urban Development's sales of multifamily dwellings that house low-income families.

Sometimes, as in the case of the enforcement agencies, the GSA may hand back a category or individual piece of property to the proprietary agency for disposal. For example, the GSA felt it didn't have the expertise to ensure safe disposal of a dam declared excess property by the Army Corps of Engineers. Worried about the dam bursting, the agency turned it back to the Army for disposal. Although the government can't afford to provide the usual warranties on the real estate it sells, it does bear the burden of ensuring that none of it would pose a danger to the purchaser or the public at large.

Another occasional supplier for GSA real estate auctions is the Federal Savings and Loan Insurance Corporation (FSLIC). FSLIC has acquired almost 2,000 properties around the country as a result of defaults on loans. They include hotels, restaurants, bars, ski resorts, ranches, condos, farms, and even a casino in Las Vegas. The FSLIC organizes most of its own real estate sales, but one interesting property it handed over to the GSA for disposal was a Lake Placid resort with sports facilities that included an ice rink where the U.S. Olympic hockey team beat the USSR team in 1980. The resort, appraised at $9 million, went for $8.6 million in a GSA auction held in 1987.

HOW GSA SALES ARE RUN

The GSA sells real property by four methods: sealed bid, public auction, broker, or negotiation. Sales normally are for cash, with a 10-percent earnest-money deposit required with the bid. When circumstances warrant, the GSA sometimes offers credit terms.

When surplus property is to be sold to the public through sealed bids, the GSA regional office concerned will mail all prospective purchasers an "invitation to bid" form containing the terms and conditions of sale, a description of the property, and complete instructions for bidding. All bids submitted by the specified deadline with the required deposit are opened and read publicly on the announced bid-closing date. If the highest bid is acceptable, an award is made, usually within sixty days, and the successful bidder is notified. Deposits are returned promptly to all unsuccessful bidders, along with notification that their bids have been rejected.

Public auctions of GSA land are conducted in the traditional manner. The winning bidder must put down a deposit in an amount that has been determined and announced prior to the sale.

The services of realty brokers sometimes are contracted to supplement other GSA sales efforts. Brokers are most often used in sales of complex industrial properties and other special-purpose properties that require an unusual effort or knowledge to round up special-interest buyers. Each regional GSA office has a panel of qualified brokers who have expressed interest in serving as middlemen for GSA sales.

Under certain conditions, the GSA's surplus-real-property sales for private use may be negotiated directly with an individual buyer or buyers. The conditions under which a sale may be negotiated are: a) when the estimated fair market value of the property does not exceed $1,000; b) where, after advertising, bid prices are not reasonable or have not been independently arrived at in open competition; and c) where the character or condition of the property or unusual circumstances make it impractical to advertise publicly for competitive bids, and the fair market value of the property and other satisfactory terms of disposal can be obtained by negotiation. This latter condition might apply, for example, to a sliver of land that is likely to be of interest mainly to owners of adjacent lots.

When the sale of a property is negotiated and its fair market value exceeds $1,000, the circumstances of the sale must be put in a written statement and submitted to the appropriate committees of Congress before the sale may be finalized.

Real property is sold by the GSA on an "as is, where is" basis. Bidders should be careful to inspect fully the property they're interested in before submitting a bid. As the GSA warns, "Failure of a bidder to be fully informed on the condition of the property will not constitute grounds for any claim for adjustment or for withdrawal of the bid."

GSA sales of real property are organized by the regional offices listed below.

GSA Regional Offices Handling Real-Property Sales

Administration of the GSA's real property sales is distributed as follows:

Region	States
Region 1 10 Causeway Street Boston, MA 02222 (617) 565-5700	Connecticut, Maine, Massachusetts, New Hampshire, Rhode Island, Vermont, New York, New Jersey, Illinois, Indiana, Michigan, Minnesota, Ohio, Wisconsin
Region 4 75 Spring Street, SW Atlanta, GA 30303 (404) 331-5133	Puerto Rico, Virgin Islands, Delaware, District of Columbia, Maryland, Pennsylvania, Virginia, West Virginia, Alabama, Florida, Georgia, Kentucky, Mississippi, North Carolina, South Carolina, Tennessee
Region 7 819 Taylor Street Fort Worth, TX 76102 (817) 334-2331	Colorado, Montana, North Dakota, Utah, Wyoming, Iowa, Kansas, Missouri, Nebraska, Arkansas, Louisiana, New Mexico, Oklahoma, Texas

Region 9   Arizona, California, Hawaii,
525 Market Street   Nevada, American Samoa,
San Francisco, CA   Guam,
94105   the Trust Territory of the
(415) 974-9086   Pacific Islands, Alaska,
                                Idaho, Oregon, Washington

You can also obtain a copy of the real-property mailing-list application card from:

General Services Administration
Centralized Mailing List Service–8BRC
Building 41, Denver Federal Center
Denver, CO 80225

Aside from regional mailing lists announcing specific real-property auctions, the GSA also publishes a national list of real estate available for sale throughout the country, along with addresses for inquiries. This "U.S. Real Property Sales List" is published bimonthly. Order it from Properties, Consumer Information Center, Pueblo, Colorado 81009. No mailing list is maintained for the publication, but there is an order form in the back if you wish to receive the next issue.

The GSA also publishes a brochure describing sales of real property to the public, "Disposal of Surplus Real Property," which you can obtain from one of the regional offices. Those seriously interested in buying federal real estate should obtain a copy of a larger booklet, "How to Acquire Federal Real Property," which explains the government's real estate sales comprehensively and includes all the pertinent federal regulations.

The GSA's Office of Finance also provides publications

about public buildings leased and owned by the government, as well as detailed listings of property owned by the United States throughout the world. Contact Public Buildings, Office of Finance, General Services Administration, Room 7106, 18th & F Streets, N.W., Washington, D.C. 20405, (202) 523-5472. The free brochure "How the Government Acquires Land" provides background info on the kind of properties the government owns. For a copy, contact your regional GSA office or Leasing Division, Office of Space Management, Public Building Service, GSA, Room 2330, 18th & F Streets, N.W., Washington, D.C. 20405, (202) 566-0638.

9

AGENCIES HANDLING FARM REAL ESTATE

FARMER'S HOME ADMINISTRATION

The U.S. Department of Agriculture (USDA) sells real estate acquired in forfeitures on farm-related government financing programs. Due to the farm depression of the mid-1980s, the USDA's real estate inventory has increased substantially in recent years, and there are a lot of bargains to be found by those interested.

The Department of Agriculture was created in 1862. Its work is to improve and maintain farm income, and to develop and expand markets abroad for U.S. agricultural products. Under that broad mandate, it has created a number of loan programs to promote rural development in many ways, from helping farmers build or buy homes to assisting industry in farm areas. Because some of the USDA's debtors are unable to meet their obligations, it has collected farmland, houses, and farm-related businesses around the country from forfeitures on defaulted loans.

Forfeited rural property is sold to the public by the USDA's Farmer's Home Administration. The Farmer's Home Administration is an agency within the USDA that provides credit for those in rural America who are unable to obtain credit from other sources at reasonable rates and terms. Like the Small Business Administration, it is a lender of last resort. It operates under the Consolidated Farm and Rural Development Act of 1921 and Title V of the Housing Act of 1949.

Loans are made by the agency's 2,200 local county and district offices, which are generally located in county seats. The loans come out of three revolving funds: the Agricultural Credit Insurance Fund, the Rural Housing Insurance Fund, and the Rural Development Insurance Fund. Many types of loans are made from these funds, covering a wide variety of property and enterprise. They include operating loans, housing loans, emergency loans, etc. When borrowers can't meet their payment obligations, either they hand over their property to the FHA, or it is forfeited by court action.

The Farmer's Home Administration has all kinds of farmlands, homes, and equipment in its inventory of forfeited or defaulted property. They run the full gamut of agricultural endeavor, including crop farms, dairy farms, fish farms, and cattle ranches. In 1987 the administration sold off in excess of 5,000 farms around the United States for a total of 1,500,000 acres. In the spring of 1988, it had 16,000 farms in its inventory.

Farmer's Home Administration property sales are conducted by sealed bid by the agency's individual state offices. The offices try to obtain at least the assessed fair market price for each property but will go lower if there are no bids.

Each state office of the Farmer's Home Administration handles its own sales. Some may maintain bidders' lists;

others do not. All sales are advertised through local newspapers and agricultural trade publications. State offices also maintain lists of all properties for sale, where they are, when they'll be sold, and where they'll be advertised. Each state capital has a Farmer's Home Administration. Just check the federal government listing in your phone directory under "Farmer's Home Administration."

FARMER'S CREDIT ADMINISTRATION

Another source for forfeited rural property is the Farm Credit Banks that are administered under the Farmer's Credit Administration (FCA). The FCA's system of banks has millions of acres of forfeited property available nationwide, due primarily to the farm depression of the 1980s.

To give you an idea of just how much property is available through foreclosures on loans from the farm credit banks, think about this astounding and little-known fact: The FCA set the all-time world record in 1987 for losses incurred by any one corporation in a given year. If you'd like to try your hand at farming or set yourself up as a country gentleman (or gentlewoman), or if you just want to get away from it all, there are some incredible bargains to be had on rural property, many of them cents-on-the-dollar buys.

The Farmer's Credit Administration is a quasi-official federal body that regulates the nation's independent farm-credit banks under the Farm Credit Act of 1971. The Farm Credit System is a nationwide network of agricultural lending institutions, which includes the nation's twelve Federal Land Banks. These banks make long-term loans through 232 local Federal Land Bank Associations (FLBAs). The FCA does not participate directly in the routine management or operations of the individual farm banks, but it has the authority to take them over when regulations of the Farm Credit Act have been violated or when it may be necessary to prevent an unsafe or unsound practice.

As for the FLBAs, they are actually cooperatives, run by the farmers they service. The money invested in the land banks is private and not guaranteed by the FCA, although it is obtained from the sale of bonds issued in federal agency markets and administered under federal government regulations.

One Farm Credit Bank loan officer told us there was so much forfeited agricultural property available in the United States in the 1980s that it was difficult to catalog it all. The majority of property is located in the Omaha, St. Paul, and Sacramento farm credit districts.

The failure of the government's farm program during the decade hit America's grain-producing areas the hardest. President Jimmy Carter's embargo on grain sales to the Soviet Union in the wake of a rapid expansion in farm spending—and borrowing—during the preceding Nixon Administration left grain farmers with a vanished market just when they'd geared up to increase production. As a result, at the end of 1986, the seventh farm credit district, for instance, headquartered in St. Paul, Minnesota, had an inventory of more than 510,000 acres of farmland worth over $246 million, all acquired by voluntary deed-backs and foreclosures.

As for California, the depression there was exacerbated by the rising cost of migrant farm labor, due to lobbying on their behalf and a step-up in detection of illegal immigrants. Fruit farmers, in particular, were hit hard; thus forfeited fruit orchards are abundant in that state.

On the other hand, Texas and the East Coast have little forfeited property for sale because these areas did not suffer very much during the farm depression. The Baltimore district, in fact, tops the nation in "liquidity," primarily because the region is pretty much one large metropolis and well covered by cement. Its truck farms have a reliable, steady income from feeding the well-off cities in the area.

The properties that are available for sale include complete farms and ranches, or tracts of land with only fields, barns, or a house on them. Some are merely tracts of woods or untillable land, because their owners needed to forfeit only portions of their property in order to decrease the amount of loan they had to service—farmers naturally turn over the least productive portions of their holdings in these circumstances.

Because they're difficult to resell, these "nonproductive" parcels can turn out to be among the best bargains for the buyer who's not interested in farming. However, some have attractions such as a cabin or trout stream on them and are well suited for personal or commercial recreation. One group of hunting enthusiasts in the St. Paul district bought a tract of nonproductive land there to use as a hunting preserve.

Many of these nonproductive parcels are small plots with houses on them. Houses without surrounding farmland are available because neighbor farmers often buy adjacent forfeited fields to increase their own holdings but don't need the house attached to the fields.

Although some of the forfeited property available is close enough to urban areas to be suitable for development, most of it, particularly in the Midwest, is of interest only to those who really want to get away from it all.

Farms are obtained by the farm-credit banks through foreclosure or voluntary liquidation, or they're deeded in lieu of foreclosure. According to law, forfeited property must be sold within three years, but the original owner has the right of first refusal before it can be sold to another buyer. It's usually in the bank's interest to get rid of property as soon as possible after forfeiture because of the costs of upkeep.

Sales of forfeited land are handled at the local level by each federal credit bank and its local offices. Methods of sale vary from district to district. Some districts hold auctions regularly; some sell property on an ongoing basis. Sacramento, for instance, has held several auctions in the past few years. St. Paul, on the other hand, has hesitated to hold public auctions for fear of driving down local land values further. Each district maintains lists of available property that may be inspected at any time by prospective buyers.

As for the prices you can expect to pay, in most cases they'll be less—sometimes *much* less—than what you'd pay for a similar "solvent" farm on the open market. A bank loses money on a farm every month that it remains unsold, because the bank receives no interest income while it's vacant, and it has to maintain the farm's insurance, upkeep, and safety. For instance, a bank might unload a farm valued at $100,000, on which it had made a $65,000 loan, for $85,000, if the farm remains unsold for as long as thirteen months, so it won't lose any more money. And in the areas where there are a number of properties available, the bargains can get pretty incredible. Sales of these properties usually are a win-win deal for bank and buyer.

When auctions are held, potential buyers must put up a deposit in order to bid. In Albemarle County, Virginia, in 1987, prospective buyers had to deposit a certified check for $75,000 before they were allowed to bid on an estate that was sold for $1.3 million. But that property was sold in the Baltimore district, where forfeited properties are rare.

The St. Paul farm-credit district, where forfeited properties are abundant, has tried to sell them in a way that does not reduce its local land values any further. But in 1987, St.

Paul felt it necessary to launch an aggressive marketing campaign because the ballooning inventory itself was depressing land values in the district. It offered "multiple-choice" loans to prospective buyers, allowing them to either write their own terms or take a 4.9 percent interest rate. Although most of the properties St. Paul has sold under the plan have gone for 110 percent of their assessed value, those assessed values were extremely low because of the saturation of the market. Their actual values were higher than priced at appraisal, since things can only get better. Why? Because the inventory of the nation's forfeited farms apparently reached its peak in the spring of 1987. Congress then passed legislation that would provide up to $1.4 billion to finance the farm-credit system so the shares held by the remaining stockholders wouldn't be devalued further. Now's the time to buy.

Prospective buyers can inquire about available property in a farm-credit-bank district at any time. A list of the farm credit bank districts appears at the end of this chapter. Organized sales are advertised in the legal paper of the community involved, and in local, and sometimes national, agricultural trade publications.

In some districts, lists of available property are compiled only at the local level and must be obtained from each local office within that district. You can also tell the head office what kind of property you're interested in, and it will notify a local office to get in touch with you.

Other districts maintain a central list available at headquarters. Several districts, such as the Sacramento district, maintain a computerized mailing list of interested buyers to whom they send periodically updated lists of available property. Sacramento's list, which is mailed to interested parties around the country, is updated monthly. It contains the information on each property's location, its owner, its acreage, the recommended selling price, and the type of commodity it produces.

A separate mailing list is maintained by a contracted auctioneer for those interested in receiving notices of upcoming sealed-bid auctions of property located in several of the districts, including the Sacramento district. You can get on that mailing list by calling (800) 822-1415.

For a pamphlet describing the organization and mandate of the Farm Credit Administration itself, write Farmer's Credit Administration, Office of Congressional and Public Affairs, 1501 Farm Credit Drive, McLean, Virginia 22102-5090. The FCA also will provide you with the list of farm-credit-bank headquarters that appears below.

Farm-Credit Banks and Territory Served by Each

Headquarters	Territory Served
Farm Credit Banks of Springfield Box 141 Springfield, MA 01102 (413) 786-7600	Maine, New Hampshire, Vermont, Massachusetts, Rhode Island, Connecticut, New York, New Jersey
Farm Credit Banks of Baltimore Box 1555 Baltimore, MD 21203 (301) 628-5500	Pennsylvania, Maryland, Delaware, Virginia, West Virginia, District of Columbia, Puerto Rico
Farm Credit Banks of Columbia Box 1499 Columbia, SC 29202 (803) 799-5000	North Carolina, South Carolina, Georgia, Florida

**Farm Credit Banks of
Louisville**
P.O. Box 32660
Louisville, KY 40232
(502) 566-7000

Ohio, Indiana, Kentucky,
Tennessee

**Farm Credit Banks of
Jackson**
Box 16669
Jackson, MS 39236-0669
(601) 957-4000

Alabama, Mississippi,
Louisiana

**Farm Credit Banks of
St. Louis**
Box 504
St. Louis, MO 63166
(314) 342-3200

Illinois, Missouri,
Arkansas

**Farm Credit Banks of
St. Paul**
Box 64949
St. Paul, MN 55164-0949
(612) 221-0600

Michigan, Wisconsin,
Minnesota, North
Dakota

**Farm Credit Banks of
Omaha**
206 S. 19th Street
Omaha, NE 68102
(402) 444-3333

Iowa, Nebraska, South
Dakota, Wyoming

**Farm Credit Banks of
Wichita**
249 N. Waco
Box 2940
(316) 264-5371

Oklahoma, Kansas,
Colorado, New Mexico

**Farm Credit Banks of
   Texas**
Box 15919
Austin, TX 78761
(512) 465-0400

Texas

**Farm Credit Banks of
   Sacramento**
P.O. Box 13280-A
Sacramento, CA 95813-4106
(916) 485-6000

California, Nevada, Utah

**Farm Credit Banks of
   Spokane**
P.O. Box TAF-C5
Spokane, WA 99220-4005
(509) 838-9300

Washington, Oregon

10

AGENCIES SELLING TAX-DELINQUENT PROPERTY

If you are interested in finding a bargain on real estate or business property, chances are good that you'll find something that will catch your eye in auctions sponsored by the Internal Revenue Service (IRS), or by local governments to settle outstanding tax debts.

TYPES OF ITEMS AVAILABLE THROUGH THE IRS

At public auctions every year, the IRS sells a tremendous amount of seized property. The past few years have seen the IRS auctioning off a great deal of unusual real estate, including a boating and recreational park, the Hollywood home of jazz great Woody Herman (which he originally purchased from Humphrey Bogart), tenement buildings that house low-income residents in Harlem, the 40-acre Beach Island, South Carolina, ranch of soul singer James Brown, and a ginger-ale factory.

But the IRS's seizures aren't limited to real estate. It also sells personal property and automobiles, and it has auctioned off such exotic merchandise as an original Georgia O'Keeffe painting (which sold for $1.9 million); the electronic gadgetry owned by convicted spy John Walker; a fleet of Rolls Royces and Cadillacs recovered from the leader of a multimillion-dollar extortion scheme; a large diamond necklace owned by convicted murderer and porn king Mike Thevis; "Hollywood" Henderson's Super Bowl ring; and a collection of antique firearms confiscated from rock-and-roller Jerry Lee Lewis.

While these are by no means the "typical" items one finds at an IRS auction, they are representative of the extraordinarily wide range of merchandise that is put on the block every year. The one thing you can count on is that when the IRS is forced to seize property for public sale, it targets real estate and individual possessions that it believes will bring in enough revenue to satisfy the claim. Consequently, you will not find piles of old clothes, broken record players, or discarded toys.

Occasionally the IRS participates in estate and bankruptcy sales, which means that both household goods and business equipment can be found at various times throughout the year. Simply put, the IRS will sell anything that is of any value to anyone. But in order to satisfy its claims as quickly and efficiently as possible, the IRS puts real estate, automobiles, boats, and other luxury items at the top of its target list.

How does the IRS come into possession of these goods? The answer is simple. If an individual refuses, or is unable, to pay taxes owed to the federal government, then the IRS is authorized by law to seize the personal property of that individual to liquidate the debt. In doing so, the IRS follows a procedure that offers the individual ample opportunity to reclaim his or her goods prior to having them placed on the auction block. At least ten days' advance notice is always given prior to seizure, and even after the federal government has taken possession of personal property, the IRS is willing to return that property if a debt settlement can be negotiated. Frequently, such settlements include establishing an installment plan for payments, or setting a grace period in which the individual in question is given an opportunity to either raise the money or sell his or her own property at fair market value. For example, friends tried to help jazz great Woody Herman liquidate his $1.6 million tax debt by staging a celebrity benefit that drew a $5,000 contribution from Frank Sinatra and a $4,000 contribution from Clint Eastwood. But the proceeds fell far short of the amount needed, and the IRS proceeded to auction Herman's property. In general, though, the IRS does not care how it gets its money and will place seized property on the auction block only as a last resort.

The IRS's main concern is with revenue, not revenge. Consequently, most of the property made available to the public is in good to excellent condition. If an IRS official thinks a specific item will not bring in much money, then it won't be seized. While it is true that private dwellings or business property may have fallen into a state of disrepair— such as the tenement buildings auctioned off in Harlem—the IRS does not attempt to mislead potential buyers. All merchandise and real estate is sold in an "as is" condition and is made available for inspection in advance of the sale. Additionally, interested parties are permitted to examine deeds, title, and any applicable business records relating to a sale that are in the possession of the IRS.

HOW IRS AUCTIONS WORK

The Internal Revenue Service is divided into fifty-eight districts nationwide, and all IRS auctions are conducted at the local district level. When private property is seized for public sale, the auction is conducted in the district where the seizure was made. Because of the unpredictability of such seizures and the time-consuming legal process the IRS must follow to dispose of property, the IRS does not have any set schedule for its auctions. Auctions are conducted throughout the year on a periodic basis, and the timing of any single sale is dependent on the time it takes for the case to work its way through the process.

One of the special features of an IRS auction is that the agency always sets a minimum price that must be met before any item can be sold. Prior to the seizure of a delinquent taxpayer's property, IRS agents determine the "forced-sale value" of the individual's personal possessions. This is used as a guide to determine what should be seized and what should be left in the hands of the indebted taxpayer. The forced-sale value of an item is always less than its fair market value, and it is used to give the IRS a reasonable approximation of how much money the agency can expect to raise from a public sale. Using the forced-sale value as a guide, the IRS establishes a minimum acceptable bid. (It is important to note that the forced-sale value and the minimum bid need not be equal. The minimum acceptable bid is usually a smaller figure.)

The IRS is not required to publish minimum acceptable bids prior to auction, and rarely does so since such a practice could result in holding bids down. If an item fails to obtain a minimum bid, then the IRS has the option of purchasing the property itself at the set price, or of returning the property to its owner. When the IRS purchases property on behalf of the U.S. Government, it usually does so with the intention of making the property available for resale or of leasing it out to an interested third party.

A second special feature of IRS auctions is that they are occasionally conducted through a sealed-bid process. This is done when the agency has seized items such as factory equipment or specialized business property that would appeal to a narrow range of buyers. Sealed-bid sales are also occasionally used when the value of a particular piece of property is so high that it would prohibit a broad public response. Luxurious yachts or large tracts of real estate could fall into this category.

For the disposal of general merchandise, the IRS conducts open-bid sales where the procedure followed is the same as at any public auction. Bids are made by hand signals, with the final sale awarded to the highest bidder.

As a general rule, payment in full is due upon acceptance of a bid and must be made the day of the auction. However, in the purchase of high-ticket items, the IRS will frequently permit a deferred payment arrangement in order to allow the buyer to obtain a mortgage loan or a bank loan. A deferral of payment is not allowed to exceed thirty days, a 20-percent down payment is required at the time of sale, and 6-percent interest is charged. In the case of closed-bid sales, a 20-percent down payment must accompany the tendering of the bid, and final payment is due within ten to thirty days of the sale.

TIPS FOR BUYING AT IRS AUCTIONS

Attendance varies from auction to auction and is usually dependent upon the location of the sale and the goods that have been seized. Whenever celebrity goods are being sold—such as Jerry Lee Lewis's antique firearms collection or John Walker's spy equipment—the publicity surrounding such an event guarantees a large crowd of curiosity seekers and souvenir hunters. It is not uncommon to see the bidding on celebrity merchandise exceed the actual market value of the goods in question. Notoriety always assures the IRS of both a large turnout and competitive bidding. Conversely, for the closed-bid sale of a piece of rural development property, or, say, a ginger-ale factory, it would not be unusual for the IRS to find itself with only one or two bids tendered. In such cases the IRS knows in advance that the property in question will not generate much public interest, and the minimum acceptable bid will be relatively low. Property of this type can almost always be purchased at a price well below its fair market value.

But before attending an IRS auction, be aware that there's a chance the auction will *not* take place—even though the IRS has gone through the trouble of seizing property, posting notices in public places, and putting advertisements in local newspapers. Federal law states that any person whose property has been seized by the IRS has the right to pay the amount due at *any time* prior to the sale. Upon receipt of such payment, the IRS will cancel pending auction proceedings and return the property to its owner. Nothing is more disheartening than to arrive at an auction site only to find an empty building with a cancellation notice nailed to the door. (Not disheartening, however, to the original owner.) This is particularly true if you have invested a couple of hours of travel in order to bid on property or an item you were eager to acquire. Therefore, a telephone call to the IRS district office responsible for handling the sale on the day prior to the scheduled proceedings can save you a lot of time, travel, and aggravation.

If you are contemplating bidding on valuable property such as an automobile, airplane, or yacht, your first step should be to determine whether or not any third parties possess outstanding claims or liens. When the IRS places a yacht or an airplane on the auction block, it is not necessarily selling you 100-percent interest in that property, but it could be selling you the interest and title rights that were controlled by the delinquent taxpayer at the time of the seizure. In the case of a Lear jet valued at $500,000, you may discover that $100,000 is owed on a bank loan which the buyer would assume responsibility for at the time of the purchase. Obviously, obtaining this information is *essential* in order to tender an intelligent bid. The IRS will provide you with all of the financial records it has at its disposal upon request, but attorneys in the field strongly recommend that you undertake an independent title search as an inexpensive, and important, form of self-protection.

HOW TO FIND OUT ABOUT IRS AUCTIONS

Pay close attention to the classified advertisements in your local newspaper for IRS auctions. The IRS is required by law to advertise its auctions in a widely circulated newspaper published in the county where the auction is to be held. In order to generate as much public interest as possible, the IRS routinely places classified ads in all of the general-circulation newspapers that are published in the district where an upcoming sale is to be made. The law also requires that a public notice be placed in the post office nearest the location where the seizure was made, and in at least two other public places in the district. These notices are required to be on display at least ten days prior to the auction, and

135

they must specify the property to be sold as well as the time, place, manner, and conditions of the sale.

An even better way to find out about the IRS auctions is to take advantage of the mailing lists that the IRS maintains in order to keep potential buyers informed of upcoming sales. Each of the Internal Revenue's fifty-eight districts maintains mailing lists for the sale of three types of goods: personal property, real estate, and automobiles. To get your name on these lists is simple, and no formal application is required. All you have to do is send your name and address to the chief of the collection division in your home district or in those districts nearby. You can request that your name be placed on any one or all three of the lists. The IRS will then begin to notify you of any upcoming auctions approximately two weeks prior to the scheduled date of sale.

IRS Auction Addresses

Write to the District Commissioner at these addresses:

Central Region

Cincinnati District

Internal Revenue Service
P.O. Box 1818
Cincinnati, OH 45201

Cleveland District

Internal Revenue Service
P.O. Box 99181
Cleveland, OH 44199

Detroit District

Internal Revenue Service
P.O. Box 32500
Detroit, MI 48232

Indianapolis District

Internal Revenue Service
P.O. Box 44687
Indianapolis, IN 46244

Louisville District

Internal Revenue Service
P.O.Box 1735
Louisville, KY 40201

Parkersburg District

Internal Revenue Service
P.O. Box 1388
Parkersburg, WV 26102

Mid-Atlantic Region

Baltimore District

Internal Revenue Service
P.O. Box 1018
Baltimore, MD 21203

Newark District

Internal Revenue Service
P.O. Box 939
Newark, NJ 07101

Philadelphia District

Internal Revenue Service
P.O. Box 12010
Philadelphia, PA 19105

Pittsburgh District

Internal Revenue Service
P.O. Box 1837
Pittsburgh, PA 15230

Richmond District

Internal Revenue Service
P.O. Box 10107
Richmond, VA 23240

Washington, D.C.

Internal Revenue Service
1201 E Street, N.W.
Washington, D.C. 20224

Wilmington District

Internal Revenue Service
P.O. Box 2415
Wilmington, DE 19889

Philadelphia Service Center

Internal Revenue Service
P.O. Box 245
Bensalem, PA 19020

Midwest Region

Aberdeen District

Internal Revenue Service
P.O. Box 370
Aberdeen, SD

Chicago District

Internal Revenue Service
P.O. Box 1193
Chicago, IL 60690

Des Moines District

Internal Revenue Service
P.O. Box 1337
Des Moines, IA 50305

Fargo District

Internal Revenue Service
P.O. Box 8
Fargo, ND 58107

Helena District

Internal Revenue Service
Federal Building, 2d floor
Drawer 10016
Helena, MT 59626

Milwaukee District

Internal Revenue Service
P.O. Box 495
Milwaukee, WI 53201

Omaha District

Internal Revenue Service
P.O. Box 1052
Omaha, NE 68101

St. Louis District

Internal Revenue Service
P.O. Box 1548
St. Louis, MO 63188

St. Paul District

Internal Revenue Service
P.O. Box 64556
St. Paul, MN 55164

Springfield District

Internal Revenue Service
P.O. Box 19203
Springfield, IL 62794

Kansas City Service Center

Internal Revenue Service
P.O. Box 24551
Kansas City, MO 64131

North-Atlantic District

Albany District

Internal Revenue Service
Leo W. O'Brien Federal
    Building
Clinton Avenue & N. Pearl
    Street
Albany, NY 12207

Augusta District

Internal Revenue Service
P.O. Box 787
Augusta, ME 04330

Boston District

Internal Revenue Service
P.O. Box 9122
JFK Post Office
Boston, MA 02203

Brooklyn District

Internal Revenue Service
P.O. Box 380, GPO
Brooklyn, NY 11202

Buffalo District

Internal Revenue Service
P.O. Box 1100
Niagara Square Station
Buffalo, NY 14201

Burlington District

Internal Revenue Service
11 Elmwood Avenue
Burlington, VT 05401

Hartford District

Internal Revenue Service
135 High Street
Hartford,CT 06103

Manhattan District

Internal Revenue Service
P.O. Box 3000
Church Street Station
New York, NY 10008

Portsmouth District

Internal Revenue Service
P.O. Box 720
Portsmouth, NH 03801

Providence District

Internal Revenue Service
P.O. Box 6528
Providence, RI 02940

Andover Service Center

Internal Revenue Service
P.O. Box 311
Andover, MA 01810

Brookhaven Service Center

Internal Revenue Service
P.O. Box 777
Holtsville, NY 11742

Southeast Region

Atlanta District

Internal Revenue Service
P.O. Box 1082
Atlanta, GA 30370

Birmingham District

Internal Revenue Service
500 22nd Street South
Birmingham, AL 35233

Columbia District

Internal Revenue Service
1835 Assembly Street
Columbia, SC 29201

Fort Lauderdale District

Internal Revenue Service
P.O. Box 292590
Fort Lauderdale, FL 33329

Greensboro District

Internal Revenue Service
320 Federal Place
Greensboro, NC 27401

Jackson District

Internal Revenue Service
Suite 504
100 W. Capitol Street
Jackson, MS 39269

Jacksonville District

Internal Revenue Service
P.O. Box 35045
Jacksonville, FL 32202

Little Rock District

Internal Revenue Service
P.O. Box 3778
Little Rock, AR 72203

Nashville District

Internal Revenue Service
P.O. Box 1107
Nashville, TN 37202

New Orleans District

Internal Revenue Service
Stop 6
500 Camp Street
New Orleans, LA 70130

Atlanta Service Center

Internal Revenue Service
Stop 29
P.O. Box 47-421

Memphis Service Center

Internal Revenue Service
AMF
P.O. Box 30309
Memphis, TN 38130

Southwest Region

Albuquerque District

Internal Revenue Service
P.O. Box 1967
Albuquerque, NM 87103

Austin District

Internal Revenue Service
P.O. Box 250
Stop 1000 AUS
Austin, TX 78767

Cheyenne District

Internal Revenue Service
308 W. 21st Street
Cheyenne, WY 82001

Dallas District

Internal Revenue Service
Stop 1000 DAL
1100 Commerce Street
Dallas, TX 75242

Denver District

Internal Revenue Service
DEN
1050 Seventeenth Street
Denver, CO 80265

Houston District

Internal Revenue Service
3223 Briarpark
Stop 1000 H-BP
Houston, TX 77042

Oklahoma City District

Internal Revenue Service
P.O. Box 66
Stop 1000 OKC
Oklahoma City, OK 73101

Phoenix District

Internal Revenue Service
2120 N. Central Avenue
Stop 1000 PX
Phoenix, AZ 85004

Salt Lake City District

Internal Revenue Service
P.O. Box 2196
Stop 1000 SLC
Salt Lake City, UH 84110

Wichita District

Internal Revenue Service
P.O. Box 400
Stop 1000 WIC
Wichita, KS 67201

Austin Service Center

Internal Revenue Service
P.O. Box 934
Stop 1000 AUSC
Austin, TX 78767

Ogden Service Center

Internal Revenue Service
P.O. Box 9941
Stop 1000 OSC
Ogden, UT 84409

Western Region

Anchorage District

Internal Revenue Service
P.O. Box 101500
Anchorage, AK 99501

Boise District

Internal Revenue Service
P.O. Box 041
550 W. Fort Street
Boise, ID 83724

Honolulu District

Internal Revenue Service
P.O. Box 50089
Honolulu, HI 96850

Laguna Niguel District

Internal Revenue Service
P.O. Box A-7
Laguna Niguel, CA 92677

Las Vegas District

Internal Revenue Service
P.O. Box 891
Las Vegas, NV 89101

Los Angeles District

Internal Revenue Service
P.O. Box 391
Los Angeles, CA 90053

Portland District

Internal Revenue Service
P.O. Box 3341
Portland, OR 97208

San Francisco District

Internal Revenue Service
P.O. Box 36020
450 Golden Gate Avenue
San Francisco, CA 94102

San Jose District

Internal Revenue Service
P.O. Box 100
San Jose, CA 95103

Seattle District

Internal Revenue Service
P.O. Box 854
Seattle, WA 98111

Fresno Service Center
Internal Revenue Service
P.O. Box 12866
Fresno, CA 93779

LOCAL SALES TO SATISFY TAX DEBTS

Local governments levy property taxes on homes, businesses, and vacant plots of land. And when those taxes go unpaid, city governments have the authority to seize the property and put it up for sale to settle the tax debt. Because local governments tend to be more active in real estate seizures than the federal government, buyers can often find the greatest number of properties to choose from by shopping at the local level.

Going through the legal process of seizing delinquent tax property is often an unpleasant chore that most city governments would prefer to avoid. In order to minimize the need to do so, many city governments conduct what are known as tax-certificate sales rather than actual property sales.

Tax-certificate sales. A tax-certificate sale is a sale where the buyer purchases the local government's right to foreclose on a piece of property rather than purchasing the property itself. Since virtually all city governments are much more interested in balancing their tax rolls than they are in brokering real estate, tax-certificate sales offer them the unique advantage of recovering overdue revenues without having to go through the headaches associated with foreclosure. That responsibility is passed to the purchaser of the tax certificate.

A simple illustration, using round numbers, will demonstrate how this process works. Let's say a delinquent taxpayer owns a piece of residential real estate that has an assessed value of $200,000. Every year the city requires that a property tax of 2 percent be paid on all residential property, and the delinquent taxpayer has failed to meet this obligation for three consecutive years. Consequently, a total of $12,000 in back taxes is overdue. (In actuality, the figure would be slightly higher than $12,000, since penalties would be assessed, but to keep things simple we will work with the round number.) At this point, the city has the legal authority to seize the property in question and sell it at a public auction. But instead of going through the legal hassles associated with foreclosure, the city decides to offer a tax-certificate sale on the property in question at a public auction.

The buyer of the tax certificate agrees to pay the $12,000 tax bill, plus any penalties and future taxes, and in return he receives the right to foreclose on the delinquent taxpayer's property. But the catch is that the tax-certificate purchaser must give the delinquent taxpayer a certain number of years (usually two or three) to pay off the tax debt and retain title to the property. In short, the tax-certificate buyer is giving the delinquent taxpayer a loan which the taxpayer can pay in full in order to remain in possession of his or her property.

All of this may seem a bit confusing, but the practice is actually straightforward and simple. Still, you may be left wondering: If the price of the tax certificate is already set at $12,000, what is left to auction? The answer is the interest rate placed on the $12,000 certificate the delinquent taxpayer must redeem in order to retain title to the property. Instead of going to the highest bidder, tax-certificate sales are unique in that they go to the bidder willing to offer the *lowest* bid on the interest rate to be charged on redemption of the certificate.

The advantages of conducting tax-certificate sales are obvious. The city government is relieved of the responsibility of seizing and selling real estate and, at the same time, is guaranteed that all overdue revenue will be collected and all future tax payments will be met. The tax-certificate purchaser knows that he or she stands to gain title to the property in question at a bargain price if the delinquent taxpayer is not able to get out of debt.

Continuing with the example used above, let's say that the delinquent taxpayer was unable to redeem the certificate, and that the only outstanding claim to the $200,000 property was $100,000 that remained on a mortgage loan. In the end, after settling the mortgage claim, the purchaser of the tax certificate would have bought $200,000 worth of property for a little more than $112,000 plus any additional taxes incurred during the redemption period. At that point, the holder of the tax certificate can turn around and sell the property for an enormous profit or retain the title for personal or business use. If the property had been sold at public auction, there is a strong possibility that the winning bid would have come much closer to the assessed value, and the bargain would not have been nearly so great.

The downsides of tax-certificate sales are equally apparent. The city government has to cope with the fact that most people are interested in purchasing real estate at the moment of the sale, and not in speculating on what will happen two or three years into the future. This limits the number of bidders and means that tax certificates frequently go unsold. In spite of its desire to avoid foreclosure proceedings, when tax certificates fail to sell, the city government is left with no option other than to exercise its right of seizure. The downside for the purchaser of a tax certificate is that when all is said and done, the buyer has tied up a sizable amount of money in a low-interest loan that yields little profit but requires a large investment of time, energy, and money that might have been put to more productive use elsewhere.

11

PUBLIC LANDS AVAILABLE
FROM THE INTERIOR DEPARTMENT

The U.S. Department of the Interior sells surplus land to the public.

The Department of the Interior was created in 1849 to act as general housekeeper for the federal government. Down through the years, however, its functions have changed with the government's growth. Its "housekeeping" duties were turned over to the newly created General Services Administration in 1949, leaving it free to concentrate on the duties of managing the nation's natural resources.

Those resources include public lands, along with energy and mineral deposits and wild animals. And whenever one of these natural resources is no longer needed by the federal government, it is disposed of as surplus in much the same way as are the government's other possessions.

The lands disposed of by the Department of the Interior are public lands. Interior distinguishes public lands from real property by defining them as undeveloped lands with no improvements, usually part of the original public domain established during the western expansion of the United States. Real property is defined as primarily developed land with buildings, usually acquired by the federal government for a specific purpose, such as a military base or office building.

Most of the public lands administered by the Department of the Interior, which comprise the majority of public lands in this country, fall under the responsibility of the department's Bureau of Land Management (BLM). Other of the nation's public lands are administered by the Forest Service under authority of the Department of Agriculture.

Most of the public lands belonging to the U.S. Government were acquired as part of Thomas Jefferson's Louisiana Purchase. The majority of them are in Alaska, Arizona, California, Colorado, Idaho, Montana, Nevada, New Mexico, Oregon, Utah, and Wyoming. Small amounts of public land are located in Alabama, Arkansas, Florida, Illinois, Kansas, Louisiana, Michigan, Minnesota, Missouri, Mississippi, Nebraska, North Dakota, South Dakota, Oklahoma, Ohio, Washington, and Wisconsin.

Once upon a time it was possible to acquire land freely in this country through homesteading, but the Homestead Act was repealed in 1976, except for Alaska, where it remained in effect until 1986. Yet it's still possible for hardy types to claim a five-acre homesite, a five-acre headquarters site, or an eighty-acre trade and manufacturing site smack dab in the frozen heart of Alaska—all for the nominal charge of $2.50 per acre, plus five frigid and very private years of squatting. But the 10,000 acres set aside for this taming program are so far back in the boonies of the wild, wild north that you have to be patient enough to wait for progress, rich enough not to need to develop the land, or pretty wild yourself, in order to profit from the experience.

The rest of Interior's surplus land isn't much better, although it's warmer. The best of America's land was claimed by the earlier settlers for homesteading, or by the Forest Service for timber management and recreation, or by the National Park Service for public parkland. What's left is either desert, range land, or precarious, most of it pretty scruffy and pretty remote. Very little of it has much productive potential. The parcels sold vary in size from just a few acres to some measuring several hundred acres. One thing about it, however—it's cheap. Although the BLM makes a point of claiming it won't sell any of it for "less than fair market value," its value is usually pretty low, because there's not much of a market for it. Only 7,359 acres of land were sold by the Department of the Interior in fiscal 1987, most of it isolated tracts. Altogether, the sales fetched about $886,800, according to one agency official.

The Bureau of Land Management can choose to sell public lands in the following circumstances: if they're scattered, isolated tracts, difficult or uneconomic to manage; if they were acquired for a specific purpose and are no longer needed for that purpose; and if their disposal will serve important public objectives, such as community expansion and economic development.

First of all, the BLM legally may sell public land only to U.S. citizens or corporations subject to U.S. federal or state laws. All sales are conducted by local offices near the land to be sold, either at BLM facilities or in another suitable public place. No sales are conducted through or at the BLM's head office in Washington, D.C.

The BLM disposes of its holdings in one of three ways: through competitive bidding at a public auction; through modified bidding where preference is given to adjoining landowners; or through direct sale to individuals, when circumstances warrant. The method of sale is determined on a case-by-case basis.

Public auctions are conducted using sealed bids, open bids, or a combination of both. In a sealed-bid auction, you need not be present to participate, but it's a good idea to inspect the property you want before you decide to buy it. Details of individual sales are mentioned in the sales notices circulated by the BLM. The notices specify the type of sale method used, the percentage of the full price you may have to deposit with each bid, and the amount of time you have in which to make full payment. If it turns out you're not the winning bidder, your deposit will be returned to you. The BLM, by the way, offers no financing.

If it's Alaska's frigid "bargains" that interest you, you have to write to the BLM's Anchorage office to find out what's left. The run on them has been pretty poky, so there's probably still some there for you. The Anchorage office will send you a map of the Alaska Settlement Area, with available parcels indicated. You simply pick what you want, then you get yourself to the site—somehow or other—and mark it out with stakes. After that, you have ninety days to get back to the BLM office and civilization to file a notice of location.

BLM sales are organized individually by the bureau's twelve state offices, so you have to write, call, or visit them periodically for info on upcoming sales. BLM sales also are advertised in local media.

The BLM publishes a pamphlet titled "Are There Any Public Lands for Sale" that describes the program and lists pertinent addresses. Request it from your local BLM office, listed below.

U.S. Department of the Interior
Bureau of Land Management State Offices

Alabama State Office
Bureau of Land Management
701 C Street, Box 13
Anchorage, AK 99513

Arizona State Office
Bureau of Land Management
3707 North 7th Street
Phoenix, AZ 85014

California State Office
Bureau of Land Management
Federal Building, Room E-2841
2800 Cottage Way
Sacramento, CA 95825

Colorado State Office
Bureau of Land Management
202 Arapahoe Street
Denver, CO 80205

Eastern States Office
(states bordering on and east of Mississippi River)
Bureau of Land Management
350 South Pickett Street
Alexandria, VA 22304

Idaho State Office
Bureau of Land Management
3380 Americana Terrace
Boise, ID 83706

**Montana State Office
(also North Dakota and South Dakota)**
Bureau of Land Management
222 N. 32d Street
P.O. Box 36800
Billings, MT 59107

Nevada State Office
Bureau of Land Management
300 Booth Street
P.O. Box 12000
Reno, NV 89520

**New Mexico State Office
(also Oklahoma, Texas and Kansas)**
Bureau of Land Management
South Federal Place
P.O. Box 1449
Santa Fe, NM 87501

**Oregon State Office
(also Washington)**
Bureau of Land Management
825 NE Multnomah Street
P.O. Box 2965
Portland, OR 97208

Utah State Office
Bureau of Land Management
324 South State Street
CFS Financial Center Building
Suite 301
Salt Lake City, UT 84111-2303

Wyoming State Office
(also Nebraska)
Bureau of Land Management
2515 Warren Avenue
P.O. Box 1828
Cheyenne, WY 82001

12

OTHER GOVERNMENT LAND SALES

DEPARTMENT OF HOUSING AND URBAN DEVELOPMENT

Some of the best real estate deals are offered by the Department of Housing and Urban Development (HUD). Property owners who have received mortgages from HUD but who end up not being able to pay their mortgage may have their property foreclosed by HUD and sold at auction. The program began in 1980, and since then HUD has held auctions throughout the United States. HUD auctions thousands of homes a year. In the Washington, D.C., area, it auctions 600 a year. (In September 1988, HUD had 47,000 homes that it had foreclosed.) By law, HUD must advertise its auctions in either the classified section or the classified real estate section of newspapers.

As with most government auctions, the homes that HUD offers range from fantastic buys to downright flea traps. Inspect your potential property carefully, and if you

1 5 3

want to bid on something, hire a professional inspector first.

Anyone can buy a house through HUD regardless of whether you're looking for a place to live or investment property. In recent years, however, HUD auctions have been mired in controversy. In fall 1988, a housing advocacy organization, the Community Family Life Services, obtained an injunction preventing HUD from auctioning any more homes unless it first "identifies which are suitable to assist the homeless" as required by the Homeless Assistance Act of 1987.

HUD mortgage auctions involve two types of mortgages, according to its own rules:

1. Assigned mortgages: These mortgages secure loans that were orginally made by the lender and insured by HUD under the National Housing Act. Lenders have assigned these mortgages to HUD after a default. The department pays insurance benefits to the lender and thus becomes the new mortgager.

2. Purchase money mortgages: These mortgages were taken back by the department in conjunction with the sale of a HUD-owned property. HUD acquired the property by foreclosing on an assigned mortgage, by taking a deed in lieu of foreclosure, or by accepting conveyance of title from the insured lender.

The Department of Housing and Urban Development has two programs for selling surplus real property to the public:

Single-family dwellings. HUD offers a full gamut of houses, listed at the local level. For more information, contact:

Sales Promotion Branch
Single Family Development Division
Department of Housing and Urban Development
451 7th Street, S.W.
Washington, D.C. 20410
(202) 755-5832

Multifamily Dwellings. HUD maintains a national mailing list at the address below, and through this office conducts sealed-bid auctions for multifamily dwellings, mostly subsidized housing for the poor. You usually buy the tenants with the building. For information, write:

Multifamily Sales Division
Office of Multifamily Financing and Preservation
Department of Housing and Urban Development
451 7th Street, S.W.
Washington, D.C. 20410
(202) 755-7220